PRAISE FOR
The Triangle of Power

"Alexander Stubb is one of the most incisive, experienced, and thoughtful political leaders in Europe today. In this book, he argues that we are at a moment in history as important as 1918, 1945, or 1989, and need a 'values-based realism' to confront the challenges that confront us from the east, the south, and now the west as well. One can only hope that Europe will listen to his advice."
TIMOTHY GARTON ASH,
author of *Homelands: A Personal History of Europe*

"It is rare for a foreign policy practitioner to write a profound work of scholarship, but Alexander Stubb has done just that. He identifies the central weakness in the international system today and has an ingenious plan to address it. It is easier said than done, but it is a crucial first step to say it clearly and intelligently, as this book does. Now President Stubb must help turn these words into action."
FAREED ZAKARIA,
CNN

"This book could not be more timely or necessary in an era of geopolitical upheaval and turmoil. Finnish President Alexander Stubb draws on his skills as a political analyst and his unique insights as a prominent statesman to lay out a path toward a new international system. President Stubb reminds us that we all have agency as citizens and offers an eloquent, heartfelt, and inspiring exhortation to individual and collective action in defense of democracy and the beleaguered ideal of global cooperation."

FIONA HILL,
senior fellow, the Brookings Institution, former senior director for Europe and Russia at the US National Security Council

"The liberal world order is dying, writes the Finnish President Alexander Stubb, for whom the Russian invasion of Ukraine was conclusive proof that the post–Cold War era was over. But what comes next? For Stubb it's a choice between 'Yalta' and 'Helsinki'—between a chaotic multipolarity and a more stable multilateralism. Only the latter, he argues, can reconcile the conflicting interests of the established Global West, the rising Global East, and the populous but less powerful Global South. But that means halting the recent decay of international institutions—a hard thing to do if the US president disparages most of them. It's even harder when the technological advances are happening in only two of three corners of Stubb's *The Triangle of Power*. This is a bold attempt at a geopolitical synthesis by one of those rare scholars who can not only talk the talk but also walk the walk in the corridors of power—not to mention play golf with President Trump himself."

NIALL FERGUSON,
Milbank Family senior fellow, Hoover Institution, Stanford

"At a moment of transition in international affairs from the post–Cold War order to an uncertain new system, President Alexander Stubb has provided Europe and the world with a precise diagnosis of how we got to his moment of disorder, and a cogent and compelling prescription for how we can rebalance and thereby create a new world order. Informed by his *dignified foreign policy* guided by *values-based realism*, Stubb's *The Triangle of Power* provides a fresh, pragmatic, and optimistic vision for a new grand strategy for international relations anchored in cooperative multilateralism, but of benefit to all in the Global North, Global East, and the Global South. At a time when illiberal nationalism seems ascendant in Europe and the United States, Stubb's clarion call for a reformed liberal internationalism is exactly what the world needs."
MICHAEL MCFAUL,
author of *From Cold War to Hot Peace*

"History hath returned, and with a vengeance. In *The Triangle of Power*, Alexander Stubb deftly argues what comes after the postwar liberal order will be determined by the struggle for power between the West, East, and South. Informed by his unique blend of academic analysis and political acumen, President Stubb makes a compelling case that the West can only secure a future guided by freedom, democracy, and cooperation if it manages to persuade the rest of the world of its merits. This book is a passionate call to action from a hardened practitioner who, despite being on the front lines of some of the twenty-first century's fiercest geopolitical battles, understands that the path toward a more stable global order runs through greater empathy rather than force."
IAN BREMMER,
political scientist, author, and president of Eurasia Group

"This is not just another book on world politics—it is the quintessential guide to the new world disorder from the ultimate scholar-statesman. In *The Triangle of Power*, Stubb delivers an unflinching analysis of the seismic geopolitical shifts reshaping today's global order. Stubb takes readers inside the corridors of power, drawing from firsthand encounters with world leaders like Putin, Trump, and Xi. Bursting with gripping anecdotes and razor-sharp insights, this is the must-read playbook for navigating the chaos ahead."
MARK LEONARD,
director of the European Council on Foreign Relations

"If I was asked to choose any leader in Europe to lead a discussion of the state of the world, I would choose Alex Stubb. He has the breadth of experience, the intellectual reach, and the clarity of thought to analyze for all of us what is really going on. His thoughts on a world moving from order to disorder could not be more timely or relevant as old certainties fall away. And his reminder that we have agency—that we can do something about the disordered world before it disintegrates—is vital advice that should help stir us all into action. This is a book that policymakers and the public need to read."
WILLIAM HAGUE,
Rt. Hon. The Lord Hague of Richmond

"Alexander Stubb is a rare, perhaps unique, figure who manages to combine the role of head of state and public intellectual. As president of Finland, he has become an important voice speaking out for Europe and describing the challenges ahead. In his new book, he describes the emerging new world order with insight and authority."
GIDEON RACHMAN,
associate editor and chief foreign affairs commentator,
Financial Times

"Alexander Stubb provides a thoughtful and challenging account of the seismic changes underway in the global order. These changes make a compelling case for an inclusive multilateralism founded on the principles of the United Nations Charter and underpinned by faithful adherence by all countries to international law. At a time when the world is confronting the existential threat of climate change, growing inequality, conflict, and instability, human happiness and progress depend more than ever on cooperation between nations and peoples. As this book makes plain, we need a world order in which the rights and interests of the vulnerable can no longer be trampled beneath the ambitions of the powerful."
CYRIL RAMAPHOSA,
president of South Africa

"Alexander Stubb's important work could not have come at a more important moment. As the world undergoes tectonic geopolitical shifts that will shape the international landscape for years to come, Alex draws on his deep knowledge of history, his expertise in interpreting global power dynamics, and his experience on the front lines of diplomacy to offer guidance for understanding and navigating today's challenging context. There is no scholar or practitioner of foreign policy better suited to bringing clarity to this complex and consequential period for the world."
BØRGE BRENDE,
president and CEO of World Economic Forum, former foreign minister of Norway

"President Stubb has presented us with a timely and compelling book about some of the most important issues we are faced with today. His case for a values-based realism and a dignified foreign policy is an insightful contribution, one which should interest all readers who want to promote a rules-based international order."
JENS STOLTENBERG,
finance minister of Norway, former NATO secretary general, former prime minister of Norway

The Triangle of Power

COLUMBIA GLOBAL REPORTS
NEW YORK

The Triangle of Power
Rebalancing the New World Order

Alexander Stubb

The Triangle of Power
Rebalancing the New World Order
Copyright © 2026 by Alexander Stubb
All rights reserved

Published by Columbia Global Reports
91 Claremont Avenue, Suite 515
New York, NY 10027
globalreports.columbia.edu

Library of Congress Cataloging-in-Publication Data Available Upon Request

ISBN 978-1-967190-10-2 (paperback)

Book design by Strick&Williams
Cover design by Kelly Winton
Map design by Jeffrey L. Ward
Author photograph by Jussi Ratilainen

Printed in the United States of America

CONTENTS

15
Introduction

PART ONE—ORDER

33
Chapter One
From Order to Disorder

48
Chapter Two
From Disorder to Disruption

63
Chapter Three
From Disruption to Disintegration

PART TWO—BALANCE

83
Chapter Four
The Global West

103
Chapter Five
The Global East

123
Chapter Six
The Global South

PART THREE—DYNAMICS

145
Chapter Seven
Competition

165
Chapter Eight
Conflict

182
Chapter Nine
Cooperation

201
Conclusions

212
Further Reading

214
Acknowledgments

Introduction

February 27, 2022. Three days into the war in Ukraine. From my home in Espoo, I am mere hours from Russia, a border that has stayed quiet for eighty years. I can scarcely believe that full-scale war has returned to the continent. It threatens to strain an already frayed world order. I send a text to Russian Foreign Minister Sergey Lavrov.

"Please, please stop this madness. You are the only one who can stop him."

Lavrov replies within a minute: "Whom? Zelenskyy? Biden?"

I've heard this line of defense from Lavrov before. This time it cannot stand.

"No. You know what I mean," I reply. "It's gone too far. History is on your shoulders."

His next text parrots the usual Russian propaganda: claims of Russian culture bans and Russians murdered in Ukraine.

I know Lavrov, and I know he's smart enough to understand what's going on. I try again.

"There is no point in the blame game. This is about life and death. We need to stop this."

No dice. Lavrov continues with the same tropes. I quit after the sixth fruitless message.

I feel angry and disappointed. More than that, I feel the tectonic plates of history shifting.

Fast-forward three years.
March 29, 2025. I stand on the first tee of the Trump International Golf Club in Florida. My playing partners are Senator Lindsey Graham, golf legend Gary Player, Fox anchor Trey Gowdy, and President Donald Trump. I used to be a collegiate golfer, though I'm rusty.

Over seven hours, President Trump and I discuss an array of world issues. I tell him what I know about Lavrov and Putin and explain why Ukraine needs to win the war. Coming from a small country, I have no illusions about outsize impact. But if I can make a convincing case that Putin can't be trusted, I've done my job.

At the same time, I understand that Trump's world is more transactional than multilateral. His presidency will change the way we conduct diplomacy across the Atlantic. More than that: it will accelerate the transition from the existing international order to something new.

Amid such upheaval, people tend to get het up. My advice: stay calm. Be a Finn. Take an ice bath, visit a sauna, and reflect. The global stakes are rising. And I am more convinced than ever that only global cooperation can contain competition and prevent broader conflict.

There are moments in history when we understand that the world is changing but don't yet know exactly where it is going. One look around the globe tells us we face such a moment now.

The rules-based world order that the West established after World War II is in tatters. Liberal democratic values are challenged by rising authoritarian powers in the East and South and populist forces within the West. Instant, universally accessible social media puts a potent weapon in the hands of political opponents plus extremist groups seeking to unravel democracy. Facts are contested like subjective opinions, truth dismissed as a matter of choice.

On the global stage, the open trading system is in retreat. The US president uses tariffs as a negotiating chip in unprecedented ways. With its America First approach, the new administration calls into question the way the US has exercised global leadership since the Cold War. This new time may indeed require new ways of thinking. But the risk of disruption and fragmentation runs high.

At the same time, China is asserting growing dominance across economic, technological, and geopolitical spheres. Russia is breaking international rules and sovereign borders without blinking. Ballistic missiles fly across the Middle East, no matter how outside nations protest. Power vacuums open and fill everywhere. Power is shifting from West to East and South, with a rising emphasis on national sovereignty at the expense of international rules. This is not the world that we in the West expected.

The trust that has been the basis of the international system has been broken. Russia's war of aggression against Ukraine was the signal that the world had changed. It showed us, clear as a missile trail, that the assumptions we rested on for decades no longer hold. The things that were supposed to bring us together—open trade, technology, energy, and global financial markets—can also pull us apart. Economic interdependence does not guarantee peace. Market economics do not assure free trade.

Liberal democracy is not a universal desire. After the Cold War, we assumed Western values were destined to become universal. Instead, they are in danger.

This is our generation's equivalent of 1918, 1945, or 1989. The next few years will decide the dynamics of the new international order for the rest of the century, or at least for decades to come. The outcome will fundamentally shift the way we live our lives. What's certain is that the world order as we know it—the power structures, relationships, and foundational principles that guide them—will be reborn. The order that emerges will depend on how we meet this moment.

The End of the End of History
The country that I am sworn to protect shares an 832-mile border with Russia. Our history books recount centuries of bloody conflict and a brutal civil war with Bolshevik meddling in the aftermath of independence in 1917. My great-great-uncle, Emil Nestor Setälä, co-authored the Finnish declaration of independence. Soviet aggression in World War II forced us to concede 10 percent of our territory, including the cities where my paternal grandparents and father were born. My maternal grandfather stepped on a Soviet mine in 1941 and almost lost his life. He met his future wife, my grandmother, in the hospital.

The timing of history made me luckier than my grandparents. I started studying political science and international relations at Furman University in the United States in 1989. When the Berlin Wall fell that autumn it felt like decades were crumbling before our eyes. Germany reunified. Central and Eastern Europe escaped the shackles of communism. The bipolar world order, a balance of power between a communist, authoritarian Soviet Union and a capitalist, democratic United States, became unipolar. The US was the undisputed superpower. The markets and freedom won. The West won. The liberal world order—with its rules, norms, and institutions—won.

I still remember the sense of excitement. There was a feeling that all of the world's roughly two hundred nations would pivot toward liberal democracy, freedom, and market economies. (Here and throughout this book, I mean "liberal" in the classical, not political sense: upholding an open society and the values of democracy, such as free speech and rule of law.) The East would join the West. The North would unite with the South. Globalization would lead to economic interdependence. War would become impossible. The world would become one. Francis Fukuyama wrote about "the end of history." I believed it.

I even took a wager, a bottle of champagne with author Jari Tervo, that Russia would become a liberal democracy sticking to international rules and norms. I lost.

Now, more than thirty years later, my job as president of Finland hinges on engaging the world as it is, not as I wish it to be. To achieve the latter, I must navigate the former.

Yalta vs. Helsinki

What the West failed to understand in those heady days is that you must be humble in victory. In international relations this means giving agency to those who lost, or more importantly those who feel they have no say in global governance. The West did not.

And so, in the first decade of this century, the world started drifting toward disorder. It became more authoritarian, multipolar, and complex. There was no longer a single leader, no clear nexus of power. America began to retreat from international responsibility after the costly failures of its wars in Afghanistan and Iraq. China emerged as a superpower through rocketing exports and economic growth. The global financial crash of 2008 delivered a severe reputational blow to the West's economic model, rooted in global markets. The US no longer drove global politics alone.

Two pivotal moments in history illustrate the crossroads at which that places us.

In 1945 the winners of World War II—the US, UK, and Soviet Union—met in Yalta, on the Crimean Peninsula. There Franklin Roosevelt, Winston Churchill, and Joseph Stalin laid the groundwork for a postwar order based on big powers. They carved up Europe into spheres of influence. Soon after, the UN Security Council arose as a platform for superpowers to address differences, with a veto for each of them but little influence for others. It was a deal made by big states over small states.

The Conference on Security and Cooperation in Europe summit in Helsinki in 1975 was different. Thirty-three European nations, plus the US and Canada, created a European security structure based on rules and norms applicable to all. They established fundamental principles governing states' behavior toward their citizens and each other. A central tenet was that all participating states had equal ability to influence decisions. This was a remarkable feat of multilateralism in a time of major tensions, and it became instrumental in precipitating the end of the Cold War.

These two watersheds underscore the difference between *multilateralism* and *multipolarity*. Multilateralism is a system of global cooperation based on international institutions and common rules—the kind of system the Allies endeavored to build after World War II, with the UN at its core. Its key principles apply equally to all countries, irrespective of size.

Multipolarity, in contrast, is an oligopoly of power. A multipolar world runs on several, often competing nodes of power, or poles. This can lead to ad hoc and opportunistic behavior and a shifting array of alliances based on states' real-time self-interest. The concern is that a multipolar world leaves small and medium-sized countries out—bigger powers make deals over their heads. Whereas multilateralism leads to order, multipolarity leans toward disorder and conflict.

Helsinki was multilateral. Yalta was multipolar. Now as a world we face a choice, and we must choose Helsinki, not Yalta. That means my fellow Western leaders and I must convince our counterparts in the many countries that the old order ignored that Helsinki has something to offer them. And we cannot achieve that by continuing to do things the way we have before.

The Triangle of Power

I believe February 24, 2022, was the day that ended the post–Cold War era. Putin's Russia, a permanent UN Security Council member, blatantly broke the rules that were supposed to guarantee peace and stability by invading Ukraine. And not only did the invasion reflect global change, it accelerated it. That day forced the world to take a position: for, against, or somewhere in between. We now see new alliances emerging in a multipolar and essentially fragmented world. The war in Ukraine became a snapshot of the new world disorder, of things to come, or of how they already were.

The core argument of this book is that the forces molding our emerging world represent a Triangle of Power—the Global

West, Global East, and Global South—and the interplay among these three will decide the shape of the world to come. These are not traditional blocs or poles, but despite their internal diversity they share similar values and interests. The Global West and East are at the two extremes. The Global South, in the middle, holds the power to decide in which direction the pendulum will swing.

The Global West is composed of the United States, Europe, and their democratic allies around the world, including Japan, Australia, New Zealand, Canada, and South Korea, to name a few. The G7, the European Union and their Pacific allies—the hard core of the Global West—represent around 15 percent of the world population and over 50 percent of the global economy. This group, led by the United States, has traditionally defended the rules-based liberal world order. Most Global West countries rely on democracy, social market economy, fundamental rights, and freedoms.

I fully admit that this definition of the Global West contains a possible weakness: the rest of the Global West will have to work hard to persuade President Trump that the liberal world order is in the US interest. Yet I do not think we should jump to hasty conclusions about deterioration of the century-old trans-Atlantic partnership. The values and interests of the Global West carry more weight than the way in which we drive them. We should also see that some elements of a Trump presidency can be useful for peace, stability, and security. He has made clear his aim of peace in Ukraine and the Middle East. Of course, how these goals are achieved—and what price is paid—matters enormously.

The Global East is led by China and supported by Russia and a set of smaller autocratic regimes including Belarus, North

Korea, and Iran. These five key Eastern countries represent around 20 percent of both global population and world GDP (both mostly China's). The Global East is challenging the current world order, seeking to rewrite the international system of rules, norms, and institutions. It believes in inviolable state sovereignty with non-interference over universal human rights and freedoms—and autocracy over democracy. Yet some Global East countries routinely question the sovereignty of smaller states. Russia, notably, wants a return to the nineteenth-century world of "spheres of influence," in which big powers make the decisions in their own neighborhood. China's military advances in the South China Sea speak to the same doctrine.

The Global South, i.e. the global majority, is broadly composed of countries from Asia, Africa, the Middle East, and Latin America. The group represents over half the world's nations and population, but less than a quarter of global GDP. India, Indonesia, and Pakistan are key Global South states in Asia. South Africa, Kenya, and Nigeria are strong in Africa. Saudi Arabia, Qatar, and the United Arab Emirates lead in the Gulf region. Brazil, Argentina, and Mexico lead in Latin America.

There are overlaps between the spheres. Many countries in Latin America, for instance, see themselves as a part of the Global West *and* South. The same goes for India and Turkey. Global South nations also are obviously diverse. They include democracies and autocracies, rich and poor states. The common denominator is that they are all underrepresented in the current world order. They lack sufficient agency and want a redistribution of power in their favor. And as everyone who wants to shape the new world order should understand, they are likely to get what they want.

Competition, Conflict, Cooperation

I argue in this book that our collective future will be forged by the prevalence and balance of three dynamics within the Triangle of Power: competition, conflict, and cooperation. Competition, at least, is a certainty, and potentially a healthy one. It will feature prominently in realms from economy to technology to military—and already does.

The emergence of conflict and cooperation, however, depend on how we manage competition. Competition among the three global spheres could spill into conflict, especially in a world where anything—from technology to energy to currency to information to trade—can be weaponized. Those same tools could become instruments of cooperation, but only if we collectively agree upon a new set of global norms and institutions to guide how we use them.

Within the Triangle of Power, each realm has its own set of interests influencing these dynamics. The core of the East-West divide lies in the geostrategic competition between the US and China: the established versus the rising power. This competition is about high politics, and as much about world order as regional power. It encapsulates an ideological rivalry between two systems of governance: democracy and autocracy, freedom and control. At the same time both camps do, at least in theory, believe in free trade and globalization. They differ on the rules and principles that should govern the system. The West, or at least a majority thereof, wants to preserve multilateral order. The East wants to rebuild the system on multipolarity.

The Global South is not agnostic about the emerging world order; on the contrary it wants agency in the system. But it does not necessarily want to take sides. A new cohort of middle powers such as Turkey, Saudi Arabia, South Africa, and India take a transactional, rather than ideological, approach. They make deals where it suits them. They decline to frame the world as simply "us versus them." To maximize autonomy and flexibility, the Global South wants the opportunity to pick and choose depending on the issue at hand, to gain fair and equal access to global goods that affect its development. And while it is not a single entity, geographically or ideologically, it wants a genuine seat at the table in governing multilateral institutions and global trade.

This explains why the Global South has remained more neutral and less engaged in the war in Ukraine. And it means that those of us in the West who believe in democracy, freedom, and cooperation cannot rest anymore on our triumphs of the twentieth century. We cannot sit this new contest out. We need to engage with our colleagues from all corners of the globe, with new creativity and humility, to determine where shifting global forces will land.

A New Prescription
As a small country living next to an imperial power, you learn that sometimes you must put some values to one side. Other times you get what you want. During the Cold War, Finnish foreign policy centered on "pragmatic realism." We had to compromise our Western values just to survive, to keep the Soviet Union from attacking us again. At times this accommodation went too far; this era in Finnish history is not one we can be particularly proud of. Therefore, when anyone suggests that a solution for Ukraine is "Finlandization," I vehemently disagree. There should be no anticipatory compliance, which amounts to giving up sovereignty.

Yet my job as president of Finland is to work with global leaders to preserve the liberal world order that can protect and sustain us all. In more than three decades in international governance, from the European Parliament to Finland's Ministry for Foreign Affairs to the presidency—managing global crises from the war in Georgia to the euro crash to climate change—I have seen how this can and cannot be done. Our path toward a steadier future starts with seeing the world as it is. And defining a way to hold our liberal values while working humbly and respectfully with those who do not share them.

I call this approach "values-based realism," and it represents a critical evolution for the Global West. Perhaps you could call it Helsinki realism. After the Cold War, Finland swiftly moved to "values-based idealism," like many Western countries that believed history was over. But after Russia's attack on Ukraine, Finland embraced values-based realism as its foreign policy philosophy. Values-based realism is not a doctrine. For me, it is an instrument of foreign policy used for a limited time, and that time is right now.

Nor is values-based realism a conflict in terms. The ideological battle of the post–Cold War era was between Francis Fukuyama's end of history (values) and Samuel Huntington's clash of civilizations (realism). Perhaps the paradigm shift we are witnessing is toward a bit of both: values *and* interests. In other words, a cooperative world order of values-based realism—rule of law alongside respect and understanding of difference.

I define values-based realism as "a set of universal values based on freedom, fundamental rights, and international rules, which take into account the realities of global diversity, culture, and history of the nation states, regions, and continents that make up the global order of international relations." A mouthful, perhaps. But its message to the Global West is to stay true to your values but understand that the world's problems will not be solved with like-minded countries alone.

The challenges we all face—demography, technology, and climate—know no borders. They don't care about autocracy or democracy, don't divide themselves according to tradition, law, or trade policy. And their solutions, if we are to forge them, will not either.

Past, Present, Future
Thousands of years ago, ancient Greek historian Thucydides identified a risk that often leads great powers into war. Political scientist Graham Allison calls that risk the "Thucydides's Trap." As Thucydides himself wrote: "It was the rise of Athens and the fear that this instilled in Sparta that made war inevitable." Over the past five hundred years, Allison counts, a rising power challenged a ruling more than a dozen times. More often than not, it ended with war.

Geopolitical determinists gloomily predict that the world again confronts Thucydides's Trap—an inevitable clash between the long-standing great power the United States and its rising rival China. A more useful perspective is to ask how we can rebalance the international system to underwrite shared security and prosperity. The Global East argues (self-servingly) that multipolarity will produce material gains for disenfranchised nations. The far better outcome is for the Global West to refashion multilateralism so that it genuinely works for everyone.

We can get it wrong, as after World War I, when the League of Nations could not contain great power competition. Or we can get it mostly right, as after World War II with the creation of the United Nations. In other words, the next decade (and consequently the next century) could go well, it could go badly, or it could go really badly. It could carry us toward a balance of power and global cooperation—or global war.

What should be clear is that in an age of nuclear weapons and AI the stakes of the race to shape a new international system are higher than ever. My text to Lavrov on February 27, 2022, was a desperate call for help, even if I knew it would fall on deaf ears. In international relations you sometimes come face-to-face with those willing to slaughter innocent people in their quest for dominance. Yet the Global West, East, and South all have an existential interest in preserving peace. Whichever supposed superpower wants its paradigm to prevail, East or West, will have to find an effective way to bring the South along with it. So far, the Global East has done this better.

This book unfolds in three sections, corresponding to the past, present, and future. The first part analyzes how we got here—the evolution from *order to disorder*. This understanding of our recent past is essential to see our present clearly.

The second part explains the present *balance* of power among the Global West, East, and South. Both democracies and autocracies grapple with similar structural challenges: demography, climate change, economy, technology, and welfare. Understanding present conditions enables us to see the choices (some uncomfortable) that lie ahead for the West.

The third part forecasts the dynamics that will shape the twenty-first century, asking *how* we can make the best of competition, prevent conflict, and promote cooperation. This is where we translate understanding into action. I contend that if the West is to maintain a central role in global power it will have to shift toward a more *dignified foreign policy* paired with *values-based realism*. A dignified foreign policy is one grounded in mutual respect, where we lead by example not exhortation. We try consistently to walk our talk of political freedom and ethical warfare, for ourselves and our allies, even when it's inconvenient. We engage in dialogue, not monologue. And we understand that we cannot dictate solutions to others.

The tasks for the West are significant and essential. We need to prevent the US-China rivalry from leading us into Thucydides's Trap, contain Russia's threat to European security, protect liberal democratic values when they are challenged, preserve an open international economic system amid intensifying geostrategic tension, confront rising populist nationalism within the West, cooperate with the East where mutually beneficial, and build a new compact with the South to refurbish the international structures that underpin it all. This is our chance to influence what kind of order the new one will be.

If you detect a sense of hope within that challenge, you should. Finns might come from the "happiest country in the world," but there is plenty of pessimism around. A Finnish saying goes: "A pessimist is never disappointed." I myself am an optimist and fan of the late Swedish epidemiologist Hans Rosling, whose book *Factfulness* promised, "It turns out that the world, for all its imperfections, is in a much better state than we might think. But when we worry about everything all the time instead of embracing a worldview based on facts, we can lose our ability to focus on the things that threaten us most." Take that to be the spirit in which I wrote this book.

We humans tend to over-rationalize the past, overdramatize the present, and underestimate the future. History is written retrospectively in straight lines but in real-time occurs in zigzags. The reality is that events of the past did not happen as rationally as we think. The present is not usually as dramatic as the buzz leads us to believe. And future changes will be even farther reaching than we imagine.

In this book, I intend to avoid those pitfalls of thinking. Instead, I want to take you on a journey that tries to make sense of the past, present, and future of global politics and bring order into a world of disorder—to understand the tectonic shifts underway so that we can push them toward the kind of world we want to live in. I want to tell you the story of how it can be done.

Part One
Order

From Order to Disorder

January 1990. Furman University, Greenville, South Carolina. I have abandoned my first major, economics, and my golf scholarship to immerse in a new obsession: political science and international relations. I study the fall of the Berlin Wall—almost in real-time. We are living history. The outcome is unwritten.

At age twenty-two, I'm hooked. I read everything I can find: books, newspapers, articles faxed from my dad in Finland. Studying the origins of the European Union, I come to believe deeply in international institutions, open society, liberal democracy, market economy, and the essential tenet that states' self-interest must be contained by global rules. As European unifier Jean Monnet said, "Nothing is possible without men [and women], but nothing is lasting without institutions."

In my idealism, I fail to understand that the West's ideological victory is going without global celebration. Many formerly colonized countries see it not as a liberation but an extension of a past they hoped to leave behind.

The lesson the ensuing decades will teach me is that all cultures and histories differ. Interests and power often supersede values. And if we want democratic values to prevail, we must correct our vision.

In Search of Order

We humans seek order within disorder to make sense of a world that often lacks it. We search for patterns and try to explain—sometimes even predict—how the world is or will become.

Our history books bear evidence of this desire. They are full of epoch-making terms that suggest some sort of order. The Roman Empire and its "Pax Romana." The Ottoman Empire. The Qing Dynasty. Defining these empires within clear narratives necessarily involves interpretation. But they nonetheless represent something concrete and critical to understand: structures that frame the relationships among populations and governments and offer a sense of coherence. We seek order because we need it.

Evolving from these regional orders came the *British Empire*, the first to extend across the globe. It was a world order, and it defined our sense of the scope of order to this day. Propelled by steam engines, gunpowder, and the telegraph, it ultimately covered almost one-quarter of the earth's land.

The *Westphalian System*, named after the 1648 Peace of Westphalia in Europe, defined our ideas about the structure of world order. These treaties established the notions of sovereignty and equality of states. World orders across history have centered on economics, trade, or cultural exchanges. But states remain the most important building blocks. Order, in this perspective, does not mean that all states are equal, but that power is distributed and managed among them to provide stability.

The assumptions underpinning our latest world order, of course, no longer apply. To understand the new rules, we need to retrace the upheavals that brought us here—beginning with the Cold War.

From Bipolar to Western Order
The Cold War defined a world that, for the West, felt rather orderly. In its simplest form it was bipolar and ideological. The United States and its allies spoke the language of democracy, capitalism, and freedom. The Soviet Union and its subjects represented autocracy, communism, and control. There was little in between (unless you count the Non-Aligned Movement of 120 states, which was neither orderly nor ideological).

Still, the two superpowers had to get along to avoid mutually assured nuclear destruction. They forged a system of joint and separate multilateral institutions and agreements for both competitive and cooperative reasons. Comecon (the Council for Mutual Economic Assistance), for example, was the Soviets' response to the Marshall Plan. The United Nations served as a joint forum of cooperation and dialogue. An array of arms control agreements aimed to limit the proliferation and use of weapons.

That feeling of order persisted even when the Cold War ended. The bipolar world became unipolar, almost overnight. Many of us, myself included, were rather quick to call the new order Western, driven by the undisputed superpower, the United States. In large part that was true. Yet even amid heady hopes, a sober look at the world would have shown us that weaknesses remained.

In reality, the 1990s were rather messy and disruptive, at least in Europe. War erupted in former Yugoslavia. Germany's reunification was rocky. The EU's enlargement, and the reconstruction of Eastern and Central Europe, took time. Russia's decade-long experiment with democracy and hypercapitalism failed. The seeds of present-day strongman rule in Russia were partly sown in this chaos.

Neither was capitalism the silver bullet to solve all problems, though it felt that way. The pendulum had effectively swung from state to market, control to freedom, authoritarian regimes to democracy. The 1990s Asian financial crisis, however, hinted at the fragility of let-it-rip globalization.

Personally, I joined Finland's Ministry of Foreign Affairs just as Finland joined the EU. Multilateralism held particular appeal for a Finn; hailing from a small country, you seek protection and amplify influence by joining forces with others. And indeed, a Westward pattern emerged as Eastern and Central European countries applied for EU and NATO membership. The choice in Europe felt clear: from disintegration to integration; from spheres of interests and submission to freedom to cooperate; from closed to open societies; from socialism to capitalism; from autocracy to democracy. The transition was imperfect and slow but crucial.

The West, we now see clearly, had an opportunity to solidify Western values around the globe then—but we did not seize it. And the changes made to international institutions were modest and mostly regional, insufficient to match the magnitude of global change.

The renamed Organization for Security and Co-operation in Europe (OSCE) added democratization and stronger human rights oversight to its agenda to guide the transition of former Soviet Republics. NATO expanded and shifted focus from collective defense to crisis-management and peacekeeping. The European Community officially became a Union, integrated further, and more than doubled its membership in the fifteen years after the Cold War. Was it messy? Of course; the pooling of sovereignty between nation-states always is.

Globally, however, the rules of critical institutions such as the International Monetary Fund (IMF) and World Trade Organization (WTO) did not change. The UN reacted to events, but its power structure remained pretty much the same—only now without a counterweight to the preeminent power of the US and its Western allies. The nations that had been sidelined remained sidelined.

The 2000s—Sliding Toward Disorder
The terrorist attack on New York's twin towers on September 11, 2001, was as tragic as it was symbolic—an attack on the two pillars of the free world: capitalism and democracy. Little did we understand at the time, but it became the moment when the long slide from order to disorder began.

The fight against terrorism became the focus of the US and much of the Western world. The attack's aftermath also revealed signs that the rest of the world would not automatically slide into Westernism—values, norms, and institutions included. 9/11 marked a turning point in what I call the West's "double mistake." One mistake was that we pivoted on our highest message, making security more important than freedom. The second was that, in attempting to direct world affairs, we gave inadequate agency and power to other nations.

The US attempt, with European interventionists such as Britain's Tony Blair, to exact retribution for 9/11 was billed by

Western politicians as the beginning of a march to democracy in the Middle East. Instead it marked the beginning of a fall to chaos in the region. Globally, the resulting entropy assured that history would not end then. On the contrary, it was about to begin.

The War on Terror presumed to thwart terrorism by force while exporting democracy to as many places as possible. It was a recipe for instability and potential disaster. Democratic change usually happens from within, rarely from outside, and never through force.

Power continued to decentralize. Talk began about the "rise of the rest" in *The Post-American World*, as Fareed Zakaria titled his 2008 book—suggesting that the real challenge to US power came not from the Cold War's losers but the winners of emerging economies. China, India, Brazil, Russia, South Africa, Kenya, and many others showed formidable economic growth. Increasingly, the rest of the world wanted a share of power, a say in the institutions setting the rules of globalization.

Meanwhile, these shifts outpaced the ability of existing international institutions to adapt to them. Much of the unease and disorder in current global affairs is about representation. Essentially: about power. So different coalitions of states, such as G7 and G20, began to challenge more traditional and multilateral forms of global governance. Patchwork cooperation was replacing a rules-based order.

As the decade rolled on, the Global West, especially the US and EU, began to look increasingly vulnerable. The US-led conflicts in Afghanistan and Iraq proved controversial and complicated. The Bush administration aimed to oust the ruling Taliban and, with a NATO coalition, create a new democratic authority to prevent their return to power. Ultimately the Taliban resurged, the West deployed roughly 140,000 troops in the region, the war killed more than 240,000 people (according to the Costs of War project at Brown University) and displaced some 6 million, and the Taliban again rules Afghanistan.

The Iraq War proved an even bigger blow to the West's credibility, especially the US. The invasion was based on a false assumption that Iraq possessed or was developing weapons of mass destruction—and occurred despite little connection between Iraq and the 9/11 attacks. The protracted conflict had no UN mandate. The superpower that had emerged victorious from the Cold War as a beacon of democratic values did not look so super anymore.

Meanwhile, the EU hardly looked like the epitome of stability either. It did grow, albeit slowly, to twenty-seven member states by the end of the decade. The widening and deepening European integration is one of its great successes. But the EU failed to become the world's "most competitive economy" as planned.

In contrast, when China set forth its quinquennial economic growth plan, it delivered. Much as it disavows a Western-designed order, Beijing has never hesitated to make use of it. Many consider China's decision to join the WTO, gaining access to Western markets, as one of the most important geopolitical events of the century so far. The global financial crisis of 2008 exposed the depth of public debt among some EU member states and plunged the Union into internal division. Europe, like the US, was distracted by its own concerns.

Personally, this decade taught me how to test my international values against the grit of reality. Representing the Finnish Ministry for Foreign Affairs I helped negotiate the Treaty of Nice, which reformed the EU structure for the accession of a dozen new countries. Through tough, long nights in 2001, we negotiated the critical question of any transnational cooperation: how to share power. And we succeeded, strengthening the EU and the states within it. Later, as advisor to European Commission President Romano Prodi, I helped develop the Treaty of Lisbon, which set forth a new EU Constitution more acceptable to member states. And finally, as Finnish foreign minister and OSCE chairman in 2008, I helped broker an urgent ceasefire in Georgia.

The phone call telling me that Russia had violated territorial sovereignty and invaded Georgia literally came when I was by the pool, on a family vacation in Sardinia. By the next day I was en route to Georgia's capital, Tbilisi, with a French delegation. In the heavily bombed Georgian city of Gori, I walked down a side street and stumbled upon women and children streaming out of buses, crying and clutching plastic bags of their belongings as Russian soldiers ordered them out. Russian forces had obviously ripped these Georgians from their homes in areas Russia wanted to claim as its own. That evening, our delegation drafted a ceasefire agreement and secured Georgian President Mikheil Saakashvili's signature. An overnight ride in armored vehicles over the mountains to Yerevan, the capital of Armenia, and then an early morning flight delivered us to Moscow, where I met Lavrov. French President Nicolas Sarkozy brought our proposal to the Kremlin, the Russians requested and received one last change, and the deal was done.

In Georgia, we managed to halt a conflict, with minimal loss of life, in just five days, through swift and coordinated international action. Yet the lesson I drew was that disorder was growing and needed to be contained. The rules that we considered sacrosanct could be broken. We needed strong multilateral institutions as much as ever. I tried to ring the alarm bells in conversations with colleagues across Europe. But the collapse of Lehman Brothers overshadowed Russia's annexation of two Georgian regions, South Ossetia and Abkhazia, as the global financial crisis began. The Global West was looking away and not looking good—opening the door to disorder.

In hindsight it is easy to say the 2000s was a wasted decade for the Global West. The US, having at last acquired all the keys to global influence, failed to stay in the driver's seat. Its financial crisis cascaded into economies across the world. The EU made a mess of the euro crisis and got entangled in internal disputes about who should foot the bill. From the outside the Global West looked arrogant, incoherent, and often inconsistent. Cooperation was fine, as long as it followed Western norms. Solidarity was necessary, as long as it caused no inconvenience at home. And international rules mattered, until they impeded the West's interests.

Nations of the Global South leveled the charge of double standards, which today has grown louder over US support for Israel as its military destroys much of Gaza at the cost of tens of thousands of civilian lives. The West spoke the language of democracy but sometimes acted with the force of autocracy.

By the end of the decade, the rest of the world had turned its back on the Global West. We just failed, or refused, to see it.

The 2010s—Disorder Arrives
The US and EU entered the 2010s in crisis mode. The emerging global sentiment was that democracy, capitalism, and globalization were not delivering. That sense only mounted through the decade as sequential crises sealed the West's fall from first place, sketching the lines of the new triangle of power.

Europe, already strained by the euro crisis, then confronted the asylum crisis. Populist movements grew across the West. The US political climate grew severely polarized. To many observers, Brexit and the first election of Donald Trump ratified the Global West's retreat as world standard-bearer. And in many ways Western voters turned their back against a world they had created. With Brexit, Great Britain became Little England. The US role as world police formally ended when it refused to respond to Syrian President Assad's use of deadly gas on civilians in 2013. Disorder had finally, and fully, arrived.

Meanwhile, China was surging from strength to strength. To people suffering under the financial crisis and questioning the capacity of democracies and market economies to maintain stability, Chinese state capitalism and control started to look more attractive. Its consecutive years of economic growth held between 6 and 10 percent. China strengthened its economic and political dependencies around the world through the Belt and Road Initiative, which invested Chinese capital to build infrastructure connecting Asia with Europe, Africa, and Latin America.

With the old world order dismantled, the pendulum of power swung widely back and forth. But authoritarian regimes—especially China—appeared to many observers to perform better than democracies.

My first phase in politics took place during the crisis years from 2008 to 2016. The euro crisis, in which several member states became unable to cover their own debt, requiring bailouts and threatening to drag the currency down with them, toppled European governments and sparked a new wave of populism. The asylum crisis, where millions of Middle Eastern refugees flooded into Europe to escape war and persecution, deepened isolationism.

As we entered the 2020s the pendulum of power not only picked up speed but started to swing in all directions. COVID-19 became a real-time measure of societies' resilience. Conventional warfare returned to the borders of Europe when Russia attacked Ukraine. The resulting energy crisis strained states' capacity to manage supply shortages. Much of it became a stress test of how states and institutions could cope with crisis. Amid the tumult, observers around the globe compared different states' mortality rates, vaccine distribution, energy prices, and inflation. The Cold War superpowers were officially off the podium, with a giant public scoreboard running numbers for their replacements.

The View from Beyond the West
We in the Global West often look at the end of the Cold War from . . . well, a very Western perspective. This chapter is a case in point. Sure, the West won the Cold War. But the deeper lesson is that world politics are never static—and if you are too focused on yourself, you fail to see your surroundings. The critical decades since the Cold War have looked very different from outside the West. And the West's myopia cost it opportunities to consolidate global influence while opening opportunities for China and others to do so.

During the West's distraction China underwent rapid economic growth and modernization, reaching de facto parity with the world's two largest economies, the EU and US. In many ways China embraced the Western recipe of economic growth through market-oriented reforms, foreign investment, and trade, but left out the element of moral high-ground. China's world was transactional; values were secondary. To many nations, China looked like a less demanding and judgmental partner than its Western equivalents, especially former colonial powers.

Meanwhile, the Middle East suffered conflict and instability, with the West's presence there serving energy and security more than democracy. The Arab Spring, starting in 2010, saw a wave of popular uprisings against authoritarian regimes but largely did not result in lasting political change. The West mostly backed the "democratic" revolutionaries, much to the dismay of non-democratic regimes with which they had previously cooperated.

Against this backdrop, many states and regions began to envision new roles for themselves. Free from bipolar or unipolar dominance, middle powers struck a more independent note in foreign policy. They could choose sides or stand back when it suited their interests. Turkey, for example—always a linchpin between Europe and the Middle East—is on one hand an ally and close partner of the West. On the other hand, it uses its size and geostrategic position to autonomously drive its interests in the region. Across the ocean, a Latin American Foreign Minister once told me, "Our region is not even competitive as a threat." The comment, by design, got a good laugh from the gathering. But it illustrates the region's wish not to be taken for granted.

India, for its part, aligns with the West on democracy and capitalism and against China's assertive strategy in the Indo-Pacific but expresses increasing frustration about its undersized role in global politics. The world's most populous country wants a seat on the UN Security Council and a greater influence in key multilateral institutions, such as the WTO, IMF, and World Bank. Already India is expanding its influence through organizations like the BRICS and G20. As a leader of the Global South, India will be a key, if not the key, state in determining whether the values of the Global East or Global West prevail.

2022—An Era Ends and an Interregnum Begins
As of February 24, 2022, we are in between eras, uncertain where the next one will lead.

The slide from order to disorder was long and multicausal, but all the elements came together on that day. International institutions and norms were damaged by a former superpower unable to find, or more precisely accept, its place in a new world order. This damage opened the door for Russia's rule breaking. Now the disorder is plain to see.

The year 2022 marks both a return to the past and potentially a new beginning. It is the end of an era of relative peace and the beginning of an *Age of Unpeace,* as Mark Leonard put it. Technology, long seen as an engine of progress, has enabled repression along with liberation, fiction along with facts. The global markets that connect us also enable economic attacks. In this world, everything from energy to currency can be weaponized. The tools of disinformation, cyberattacks, and sabotage equip nations to blur the line between peace and war. This is what makes disruption more dangerous and the establishment of new global rules more important.

The Global East wants to frame this moment as a reckoning on the Global West's hegemony. The Global South wants to frame it as a reordering of global power and goods to better reflect the present world—and it is probably right.

The paradox is that no matter where you are in the world, your conditions are being rapidly reshaped by the same key structural forces of change: demography, climate, and technology. You can't escape them. No country can. All three forces penetrate the dynamics of local, national, and international governance. And all eventually cause disruption, fragmentation, and imbalance—issues with which all regimes, West, East, or South, must contend.

At this watershed moment, the trending political rhetoric is exactly at odds with the solutions we need. Global leaders talk of nationalism, taking back sovereignty, or putting their people first. Yet interdependence now is a critical part of the solution, not the problem.

What will the next era be called? Defining an era is as difficult as determining when it ends. Tyrants can seem all-powerful until the moment they are not, as we saw when Syria's Assad was scuttled out of office in a matter of weeks. It is safe to say that the post–Cold War era is over, but the new era's identity is not yet clear. For now, I will call this stage an *interregnum*, an in-between period where disruption rules.

To glimpse our global direction we have to detach from the day-to-day mayhem of world politics—which is not that different from the financial markets' ups and downs. There is always something happening, but not all of it is ultimately important.

It is tempting to conclude that the future will see a bipolar balance between a US- and EU-led liberal order and a Chinese-led authoritarian order. I think this is too simplistic, because it assumes that we live in a binary world of alliances. We do not. It is more likely that we will see flexible alliances—essentially a regionalization and decentralization of world order. These alliances will be based on values, interests, and necessity— a push-pull of forces that this book will explore.

To imagine this evolution, we first need to fully understand its tipping point: the 2022 Russian attack on Ukraine. That moment shows us how different players are positioning themselves in an interregnum—and illuminates the foundations of the new world order and our opportunity to help build it.

From Disorder to Disruption

February 24, 2022. I wake up in Florence at 4:00 a.m. for an early flight to Helsinki. I open my news feed—and can't believe my eyes. Putin's Russia has attacked Ukraine. There is full-scale war in Europe.

I walk outside, past stone buildings nearly a thousand years old. Observers expect Russian forces will breach Kyiv within forty-eight hours and topple the government.

On the plane, I scribble in my notebook: "Georgia in 2008. Crimea in 2014. This is now the third invasion by Russia in fourteen years." Yet unlike Georgia, this conflict changes everything, for Finland, Europe, NATO, and the world. I write: "This has to be the tipping point. A power in decline is dangerous. Russia proves the case in point."

Especially sobering to me is that I have met many of the people behind the war and have heard firsthand the lies that justify it. I know these people's intelligence. I did not anticipate their disregard for peace.

Within days, most countries will condemn Russian aggression at the UN (141). Others will abstain (35). Only a handful will support (5).

But most significantly, only 40 of roughly 200 member states will ultimately sanction Russia (condemnation is words, sanctions are action). None from Africa and Latin America. Only a handful from Asia.

On the eve of the Russian revolution Vladimir Ilyich Lenin reportedly said, "There are decades where nothing happens, and there are weeks where decades happen." I rarely agree with communist revolutionaries, but on this one, comrade Lenin was right.

If Lenin were still alive he might update his observation and say there are also decades when centuries happen, when long futures are written in short years. Such a decade begins on this day.

Immediate Reactions to War

My notes from February 24, 2022, suggest that after the initial emotion, my brain went into rational overdrive. I talked with politicians, military experts, diplomats, and journalists in Europe and the US, taking notes, organizing my thinking. The notes now reveal that most of these people were genuinely scared. Some understood they had misread Russia. Others knew their foreign policies had to change.

Among my Finnish compatriots, the fear was palpable. For us the attack brought back our grandparents' warnings about Soviet aggression and their memories of World War II. We had maintained one of the largest armies in Europe, but many Finns suddenly realized that staying out of NATO was a potentially existential mistake. At the same time Finland's strategic importance grew exponentially as Western allies eyed the potential escalation of the conflict toward the Baltic Sea, which touches Finland's shores.

I found myself interpreting the Finnish perspective in international media, giving around five hundred interviews in a few months. As a professor then, academic freedom allowed me to say things political leaders could not. Government experience helped me understand what was going on in the engine room. My off-the-record conversations gave me all the information I needed to read beyond the headlines. I corrected misperceptions about Finnish "neutrality" and calmed fears that we were next in line. I knew Russia would not have the capacity to act on two fronts. I also saw quickly that Finland would finally seek NATO membership.

What I did not realize until my exchange with Lavrov three days in was that, unlike Georgia in 2008, this war was beyond the point of no return. Russia would not back down and Ukraine would not give in. And the war would upend what remained of the old world order.

To understand the dominoes that began to fall then (and continue now), we must cut through the emotion and examine *why* Putin decided to attack Ukraine—and from there, why different states reacted as they did. These reactions, even those which disappointed the West, were rational from each state's perspective. For some it was about political security. For others it was about energy and food security. For everyone it was about their place in the world.

Putin Is Not Crazy
When the war broke out, Western media was full of speculation about Putin's mental state. I had met Putin several times. (Since the Ukraine invasion and since I became president, I have not spoken to or seen him, by choice.) My impression from those meetings is different than the psychoanalysis provided by Western pundits, most of whom have never met him.

The last time I met Putin was September 2013, when he and then Finnish President Sauli Niinistö opened a power plant in Siberia, a €2 billion investment between our two countries. The meeting was scheduled in the afternoon, to be followed by dinner. Putin, famously and chronically late, arrived at 11:00 p.m. Dinner followed at midnight (notably served by chef Yevgeny Prigozhin, who would later lead the militia that marched on Moscow to overthrow Putin in 2023.) Now that same power plant has been confiscated by Russia and its status is in arbitration.

Putin was, as always, well prepared, analytical, strategic, and composed. We conducted entirely rational conversations. He showed empathy. He smiled wryly and appeared to really listen. He knew how to take the room, so to speak. And I see no reason to believe that anything has changed.

What is lost on those who believe Putin crazy is that the world looks different from the Global East and South than from the West. What appears insane through one lens may look rational through another. And to effectively navigate a changing world, we need to see through both.

The rationale for the attack on Ukraine is more complex than critiques of Putin's mental state suggest. Russia has its own historical narrative, as deeply rooted in Russian culture and education as the American Pledge of Allegiance in the US. In this narrative, Russia has always been threatened, alone, and isolated, attacked from all directions, whether by the Mongols, Nazis, or NATO. This story holds that Russia has a mission to preserve true European Christian ideals, which the West has abandoned with its decadence, and that only Russia has been able to defeat those aiming to conquer and control Europe, like Napoleon and Hitler. These are mainstream views in Russia, not only cheered in the margins. There is nothing innately wrong with building that national identity. There can, of course, be problems with how it is applied.

Through this lens we should also understand that Russia never accepted the post–Cold War liberal order. Russia believes in big power politics rather than multilateral cooperation. Foreign relations for Russia have always been a zero-sum game ruled by strength, not norms. There are no values involved. If you win, I lose. If I am bigger, I decide. The Soviet Union is still seen as part of Russian greatness.

Putin promotes a revisionist vision of Historic Russia. His *Russkiy Mir*, or *Russian World* doctrine, is about one language (Russian), one religion (Orthodox) and one leader (Putin). This forms the ideological basis to justify control of post-Soviet territories with Russian puppets or proven friends of Moscow. For Putin the Soviet Union's collapse was a travesty, and Stalin was a hero. Putin wanted to Make Russia Great Again—this is his mindset, not his medical state, and it is widely shared in Russia.

In that spirit, Putin laid bare his longstanding obsession with Ukraine as part of Russia in a July 2021 essay that practically denied Ukraine's statehood. His aim is to rebuild the Russian empire. And as Zbigniew Brzezinski once observed, without Ukraine, Russia ceases to be an empire.

Putin's attack on Ukraine will, nevertheless, go down as one of the biggest tactical and strategic blunders of modern history. He thought Ukraine would fall into his arms in a matter of days. After all, that was how easily he claimed parts of Georgia and annexed Crimea. But tactically he overestimated Russian military capability and underestimated Ukrainian resistance and Western resolve. Strategically he achieved the opposite of what he expected: Ukraine became more European than Russian, the EU and US grew more united, NATO returned to its founding purpose, and Finnish membership doubled Russia's border with NATO. He also forgot that to succeed in war you need not only tactics and strategy, but a sound reason to engage. If an invasion could not control the minds of Ukrainians, Putin could not expect to control Ukraine.

Once Putin invaded, however, the war was too big for him to fail and keep his position. Being wrong is not necessarily crazy. Nor is being disastrously self-centered and stubborn.

What Putin got right was the domestic reaction. Anti-war protests remained small and met a furious crackdown. The few loud opposition figures were effectively driven out of the country. Almost no one else was brave enough to publicly object. The result became a fight for Putin's existence. He wanted a place in history next to Peter the Great, Catherine the Great, and Stalin, but might end up closer to Tsar Nicholas II, who abdicated amid anger over territorial losses, massive war casualties, economic difficulties, and domestic turmoil.

Why hasn't Putin's inner circle pushed back? We Westerners are often bemused to see the Russian leader giving orders to governors and oligarchs in public, but in fact these performances reflect the way Russia has always been ruled.

Russia is a conservative society. It hates disorder. From the times of Ivan the Terrible in the 1500s to today, it has been ruled by authoritarians. The Tsars had God-given rights. The Communist leaders drew legitimacy from the class struggle. The disruptive 1990s of hypercapitalism and democratic transition engendered disorder, which Putin stabilized when he rose to power. For many Russians the word *democracy* still equals chaos.

Correspondingly, Russians have dubbed that democratic experiment *dermocracy, or shitocracy.*

Now, governors may rule a region or city—and oligarchs may manage a company or industry—for as long as the leader is pleased with their performance. The leader's power rests on loyalty among the elites, and as such leaders are almost never bound by political institutions or law. They are never wrong. Neither are they accountable to the people. In this system of organized corruption, we should assume that most of the political and economic elite back Putin, at least until things go sour and the oligarchs and governors lose out.

In other words, power, order, and Russian hegemony have been foundational values in Russian culture for centuries, and the Ukraine invasion is consistent with that point of view. It was only crazy by Western reasoning. With this understanding, we should also assume that Putin will go all the way.

Am I a deterministic doomsayer claiming that Russia will never change? Absolutely not. I have enough Russian friends and experience to understand that not everyone reveres their *Russkiy Mir* leader. But change in Russia often necessitates a people's or palace revolution, and both appear very unlikely now.

From the Global West's perspective, the good news is that Putin failed. Unless his strategic aim was to Europeanize Ukraine, unify the EU, revitalize the Transatlantic partnership, and drive Finland and Sweden into NATO. In the process he destroyed the Russian economy and alienated himself from many allies. Russia used to be able to blackmail Europe on three fronts: economic cooperation, energy dependence, and military might. The first two do not feel particularly threatening anymore, but we should never underestimate Russia on the third.

The United Global West

Alongside the misery Putin's failure sowed in Russia and Ukraine, it set in motion a chain of reactions that will eventually remake structures across the world. Let's examine those, starting with the Global West.

In my thirty-year career in international relations, never except after 9/11 have I seen the Global West more united, determined, or effective than in the immediate aftermath of Russia's attack. Nothing unifies more than a common enemy. As Russian bombs fell on Ukrainian cities, the West collectively launched coordinated declarations condemning the war, consecutive waves of unprecedented sanctions, strategic military and financial aid, massive demonstrations, operations to house refugees, and waves of sympathy.

The West responded with such clarity because, quite simply, we had to. For many of us a Russian attack is existential. The US, EU, and NATO needed to show unwavering unity against this threat. Europe even overcame two mistakes that critics claimed it made in the post–Cold War era: counting on American security and depending on Russian energy. Perhaps those mistakes were real, but Europe was able to rely on the former and wean itself from the latter when it mattered.

The ripples of that response spread across Europe and the Atlantic. As the EU united, Russia's neighbors turned their back on Moscow. Georgia, Ukraine, and Moldova applied for EU membership. (Georgia later suspended its application.) Forty-four European states, including Armenia and Azerbaijan, joined a first meeting of the European Political Community in Prague in October 2022. The only ones not invited? Russia and Belarus.

This revived unity could prove a crucial asset amid the present disorder, and we should strive to sustain it despite differences with the new administration in Washington. We need it now especially because Russian aggression produced an apparent contradiction for the West. In one respect, it was fresh proof that an international order based on common norms and institutions is better than rogue behavior. Yet it simultaneously forced the West to recognize the weakness of these norms and institutions on the world stage. Global responses to the West's attempts to sanction Russia have ranged from lukewarm to neutral.

The upshot is that the West must go back to the drawing board and decide how it can best defend its interests and maintain at least some parts of a liberal world order. The reflection begins with an understanding that most of the world's nations will not automatically follow in the West's footsteps—a fact of which the Global East is increasingly aware.

The Reluctant Global East

A few weeks before the war began, Presidents Xi Jinping and Vladimir Putin met at the Beijing Winter Olympics. In a joint declaration, China and Russia stated that "friendship between the two states has no limits, there are no 'forbidden' areas of co-operation." Read that as you will.

It is impossible to know whether Putin told Xi about his intention to attack Ukraine, but once it happened China landed in an uncomfortable position. Had the attack succeeded, things might have been different. China illustrates the Global East's balancing act in the present disorder: it wants to unseat the West from dominance but is reluctant to do so in a way that potentially damages its own interests.

For China the war was both a distraction and an opportunity. Xi would have preferred all eyes on his dominance of the Chinese Communist Party quinquennial congress in October 2022, through which he secured an unprecedented third term as president. He also wanted attention and admiration for China's zero-COVID policy (which was initially successful but outlived its purpose and ended up costing China and its citizens dearly). The war was not part of China's five-year plan. The opportunity, however, was for China to cement its dominance over Russia as the real leader of the Global East—which it did.

China's strategic calculations unfolded cautiously. At first it sat on the fence. But as the war stretched on, China had to confront three options: lean toward Russia, lean toward the West, or stay neutral. Whereas the Russian economy doesn't matter much to China, except as a source of raw materials, the EU is one of China's biggest trading partners. This gave China genuine reason to worry about secondary sanctions if it backed Russia overtly. So it ended up choosing to balance all three options, to juggle its competing interests rather than sacrifice one.

I have met Xi Jinping three times, most recently in 2024. I always find a respectful dialogue more fruitful than a disrespectful monologue, especially if you disagree. So I took care both to listen and to explain why Russia's attack on Ukraine was wrong and how its ramifications affect global security. Xi was personable and well-versed in his subjects. He adeptly analyzed world-scale questions about technology and global goods but did not engage about matters he considers China's private business, like human rights.

The conclusion I drew is that China's and Russia's "friendship without limits" means less than we think. For China it is transactional. For Russia it is necessary. It is an alliance more of convenience than of depth. Both nations want to usurp power from the West. They share a common enemy: the US and to a lesser extent the EU. Each leader wants the other to remain in power to bolster his country's position.

But it is important to understand that the two powers' goals and methods differ. Russia is an aggressive disruptor seeking to secure a sphere of influence. China is a global economic superpower, and as such it cares about its reputation. Hence its attempt, albeit clumsy, to mediate peace one year into the war.

Beyond China, the war began to upend many previous patterns. Iran, for instance, intensified its cooperation with Russia, supplying it with arms and drones. North Korea has sent supplies and even troops to fight with Russia in Ukraine, flying in the face of China's aim to prevent escalation. Since 2022, many Central Asian countries have distanced themselves from Russia, indicating that whole regions can quickly shift alliances. Yet this means they can, just as quickly, shift back.

The year 2022 also delivered hits to China's reputation in both governance and economics, as its COVID-19 approach backfired, its strategic relationships stumbled, and its growth slowed—showing a weak side the world had not seen for three decades. Those optics are sure to linger and affect the emerging world order.

Ultimately, the Ukraine war will probably recalibrate the East's relationships with its diverging leaders, China and Russia, and prompt China to reassess where to find friends. It will also force China to rethink any possible ambitions on Taiwan. The opportunity cost of Putin's senseless war is too high. I think President Xi understands that—but I could, of course, be wrong.

The Neutral Global South

The Global West sighed with relief when 141 UN states voted to condemn Russia a few days into the war. But behind the scenes, many of those votes were soft—scrambled together at the last minute by the US, EU, and their allies, often with a transactional exchange. The 35 abstaining members, including India, China, and South Africa, represented over half the world's population. The four countries that supported Russia—Syria, Eritrea, North Korea, and Belarus—were less of a surprise.

Many in the West mistook the vote for an overwhelming expression of support. This interpretation was too early and too optimistic. Only about forty countries were ultimately willing to translate those words into action by sanctioning Russia. The reason was not indifference but dissociation—a sentiment that this is "your war, not ours." The conflict may have had global repercussions—such as inflation on fertilizers, food, and energy—but it fundamentally concerned Europe. Many states felt that the West, especially former colonial powers, were in no position to lecture on territorial integrity, sovereignty, or independence. Indian Foreign Minister Subrahmanyam Jaishankar expressed a widespread Global South view when he remarked in 2022, "Europe has to get out of the mindset that Europe's problems are the world's problems but the world's problems are not Europe's problems." And he was essentially correct.

Overall, the South's reaction had less to do with the war in Ukraine than with their role in the global order. Middle powers, as aspiring great powers, now have greater scope to make their own choices.

Take India, the leader of the Asian Global South. It has sat on the fence since the war began. Looking through the lens of security and big power politics, we see that India is a member of the Quad, a diplomatic partnership with the US, Australia, and Japan—and one of the biggest arms importers from Russia. It needs to manage a historical conflict with Pakistan and keep a wary eye on China's regional power. Its balancing act is not only understandable, but for all intents and purposes has been successful.

Latin American countries mostly supported Ukraine in words but defended non-intervention in actions. In Brazil, both the right- and left-wing presidential candidates, Bolsonaro and Lula, blamed NATO's expansion for Russia's attack—moving beyond simple neutrality to a kind of equal-opportunity critique. The lesson was that, rather than take sides, Latin America prefers to keep its options open.

It is unfair to generalize about the African Union, composed of fifty-five states, but safe to say that reactions were at best neutral. This is, first, because African leaders tend to see Russia as a more constructive and less demanding partner than Western states, especially those with a colonial past. Second, because many African states have close economic ties with Russia, especially in food, energy, defense, and in their fond memories of Soviet support. And third, because Africa has a tradition of non-alliance in big power competition.

The theme running across regions is that debates in the Global South hinge on interests, which tie into political or economic commitments to both the Global West and East. And they manifest in flexible, rather than rigid, alliances. These countries see themselves as rightful actors on the world stage, and they're not keen to do anything that would constrain their ascension.

From Fragmentation to Reconnection

Sometimes we humans suspend the truth for survival. Memories fade so that we can move forward. Order itself is a mental construct or theory. Disorder is often reality. Yet history does provide moments of disruption that crystallize broader trends of change. The war in Ukraine was one of those disruptions.

When I began writing this book in early 2020, I thought about how to frame the emerging world order. The narrative of a bipolar Cold War, then a unipolar—and later multipolar—post-Cold War came easily. But what then?

In an earlier version of the book my framing was bipolar, driven by two power centers: China and the US. Yet as history charged on through COVID-19, Ukraine, and the energy crisis, I realized the world was not as orderly as I wanted to believe. The world order was a cacophony of disorder, with hundreds of relationships ranging from global multilateral institutions to regional groups to informal connections between companies, states, and civil society.

It was, at last, the Ukraine invasion that solidified these lessons for me—that remade my understanding of the world and led me to declare the old world order officially dead. We are not simply in a transition; we are in a fight for a future world order. And the path to a healthy outcome necessarily runs through international institutions, from the UN to settings far beyond it, where we must rethink membership and power for global cooperation to survive.

As new alliances formed and crumbled amid crises, and multilateral institutions such as the UN and OSCE were sidelined in the Ukraine invasion, some pundits announced the death knell of international institutions. I disagree. These institutions are more resilient than we often think. And they will prove critical to reshaping the relationships of our evolving world.

From Disruption to Disintegration

September 2008. World leaders gather in New York for the UN General Assembly. Lehman Brothers has just collapsed. Markets are in turmoil. I am Finland's foreign minister and chairman of the OSCE.

My calendar is full of one-on-one meetings. Each country has its own priorities. Many colleagues want my take on the frozen conflict in Georgia. I want to secure Finland a rotating seat on the Security Council.

At an EU ministerial lunch, Sergey Lavrov comes in late. Takes the microphone. Starts rambling about how Georgia attacked first. We all know he's lying.

To an outsider, this scene may look like a flurry of formality among elites, far removed from reality. But it is the foundation on which we build a multilateral, rules-based world order and seek common solutions to common problems. Even spontaneous conversations in the hallways can seed trade agreements, climate pacts, or military alliances.

Relationships between countries ultimately rest on relationships between people. Diplomats build rapport because a hard conversation is better than a chasm of silence, and a compromise is better than no agreement at all. And once we know each other, we know who to call for support when a climate disaster hits our shores, a new energy opportunity opens, or a missile lands where it shouldn't.

I know firsthand that multilateral diplomacy can be messy. But we cannot rebuild a world order without it.

The Currency of International Relations

I have always loved international gatherings, from academic conferences to the UN General Assembly, from the Munich Security Conference to informal retreats. Formal sessions afford a chance to pick up signals on the direction of negotiations at hand. In informal exchanges outside the meeting room—often where the real work gets done—we forge personal connections and feel the world's pulse.

Believe it or not, there are more than 50,000 international fora, summits, networks, institutions, and organizations that channel international cooperation. They may be formal or informal, governmental or non-governmental. Think, for example, of India's Raisina Dialogue, Singapore's Shangri-La meeting, GLOBSEC in the Czech Republic, the World Health Organization, and the World Economic Forum. Together they make up the international system we know today and give rise to the agreements, structures, and rules that comprise our world order. The bonds they build between countries—and the shared ideas they foster—are critical to peace and cooperation. (For the same purpose, I made a point to meet nearly half the world's state leaders within my first year as president.)

These international fora have never been more important. Yet many countries are rejecting multilateralism when we need it most. In fact, the fraying of global structures has helped drive us toward disorder. Without strong multilateral systems, all interstate deals become transactional. A multipolar world runs on self-interest. A multilateral world makes the common interest a self-interest.

Rising multipolarity has set in motion three trends—multiplication, regionalism, and distrust—that complicate our prospects for rebuilding a world order today. The first two, multiplication and regionalism, are challenging but not necessarily unhealthy for a liberal world order. The third, distrust, is our biggest obstacle to overcome.

The UN: Still the Backbone of the World Order
To revitalize multilateralism we need to understand how it has evolved and devolved. Let's begin this history with World War II.

The Soviet Union, United States, France, and Great Britain called their military alliance the "united nations" long before the global organization began. Forty-two more countries signed on during the war. At the Conference of San Francisco in April 1945, fifty-one states spanning every inhabited continent created the United Nations to underpin a new international system meant to prevent another global conflagration. Almost all of Latin America and several Middle Eastern countries were founding members. So was India, even before attaining formal independence. Much of Asia and Africa had yet to emerge fully from colonial rule. The UN became the backbone of the rules-based world order. Its single most important task: keep the peace.

A lot has changed since 1945. One of the UN's founding members, the Soviet Union, no longer exists. Dozens of nations have broken free from colonialism and forged their own governments. The UN's initial 51 member states have grown to 193. Other international institutions have proliferated. Critics rightly point out that the UN's core structures have not kept up with change. But the UN remains the cornerstone of the multilateral world order, and we dearly need it—even if we need to make it better.

A stronger UN starts with a more balanced Security Council. The Security Council holds the institution's primary responsibility, "the maintenance of international peace and security," and the global monopoly to authorize the legitimate use of armed force under international law. Yet its leadership is unbalanced. With the dust still settling on world war in 1945, the four allies plus China received privileged status with permanent Security Council seats and veto powers (the remaining ten seats rotate among nations). Nothing could happen against the permanent members' will. In return, they stayed engaged. This original design reflected the power dynamics of the day: a balance between the Global West and Global East. The Global South was, and still is, left out.

The UN expanded over time, setting up a growing portfolio of activities from supporting economic growth to protecting the environment to fighting hunger to resettling refugees. Through the Cold War, it mostly managed to keep peace on a global scale. It is to date the most universal, inclusive, and far-reaching attempt at global governance the world has seen. Its institutions, rules, and practices became the foundation of an international system that grew exponentially after 1945: the *Yearbook of International Organizations* counted 123 intergovernmental organizations in 1951, and over 1,800 in 1990.

Today, the UN is no utopia. No world war has erupted since its founding, yet it has proven unable to contain the rising belligerence of nation-states. It is, like most international organizations, driven by its members' conflicting interests. To paraphrase Winston Churchill on democracy: the UN is the worst form of global governance, save all the others.

There are three primary criticisms of the UN in its present state. First, many lament its inefficiency, and they do not only mean the elevator operators that take you up and down during the General Assembly. As a large bureaucracy navigating multicultural environments and diverse interests, UN structures are not built for fast decisions or smooth processes. Many think the UN fails on its main missions, from development to conflict prevention to mitigating global warming. Yet most forget that international organizations are never perfect, especially those with 193 members. The UN works about as efficiently as you can expect when the world tries to negotiate with itself.

Second, the UN is often accused of encroaching on national sovereignty. Concerns range from the conditionality of IMF and World Bank financial aid, to UNESCO policies on schoolbook design, to UNHCR human rights reporting obligations, to the Responsibility to Protect (a requirement that every member state protects its population from crimes against humanity and the international community steps in when needed). Not only authoritarian regimes but also democratic actors have scolded the UN for decisions they saw as incompatible with national laws, values, and interests. They conveniently forget that the UN's purpose is to solve problems beyond the remit of any national government alone.

Third, despite the UN's democratic pretense (e.g., through the "one state, one vote" principle in the General Assembly), critics have attacked the UN for perpetuating global power disparities. Global South countries contend that it mainly represents Western values. Even during the Cold War, the Non-Aligned Movement depicted the UN as great power talking shop, rather than a democratic institution addressing the world's inequalities.

This view deepens when vetoes by the Security Council's permanent five limit the UN's scope of action in crisis. Newly emerging powers remain eclipsed from the world's most consequential decision-making body. This view unites not only Global South countries such as India, Brazil, Nigeria, or South Africa, but also Global West countries including Germany and Japan.

Even with its flaws, the UN is still by far the world's most important international institution—the spider in the middle of a complex web of international institutions—and must be a central player in the effort to build a new world order. The critical step is neither to keep the UN stagnant nor to abandon it, but to make it work better for all members. And that starts with agency—reforms to ensure that most of the world is properly represented and its interests met. Many nations would rather work through the UN than through shaky bilateral relationships. But they need a genuine voice there to engage.

An Opportunity Lost

The end of the Cold War was a prime opportunity to revitalize the international system. Competition was over. Cooperation was on the menu. Global conflict seemed unlikely. With the battle between the two heavyweights resolved, the rest of the world stood ready to step into the game.

Early signs looked hopeful. When Saddam Hussein invaded Kuwait in 1990, the former Cold War rivals jointly condemned the aggression. The UN Security Council, in surprising unanimity with Cuba and Yemen abstaining, imposed several rounds of sanctions, then authorized the use of force to expel Iraqi troops from Kuwait. By the end of February 1991, a military coalition led by the US and backed by the Soviet Union, including Egyptian and Saudi Arabian forces, defeated Saddam's troops and ended the First Gulf War.

I remember watching US President George H. W. Bush's speeches on the "new world order" as a student at Furman University. The Gulf War, he said, was about "more than one small country; it is a big idea; a new world order." Exciting stuff for a young student of international relations! In another speech Bush spoke of "new ways of working with other nations to deter aggression and to achieve stability." Emerging from the Cold War stalemate, it seemed the United Nations could finally live up to its founders' ambitions.

What unfolded, however, was nearly the opposite—an international devolution that drove fragmentation, not consolidation, and accelerated the slide from multilateral order to multipolar disorder.

The Global West took steps at first to strengthen international systems. The early 1990s was busy with international institution building. The Conference on Security and Cooperation in Europe (CSCE) was strengthened and consolidated into the Organization for Security and Co-operation in Europe (OSCE). The European Communities became the European Union, set on deepening economic ties and expanding eastward. NATO incorporated a reunified Germany and eventually most of the former communist states of Central and Eastern Europe. The World Trade Organization (WTO) emerged, joined by many post-Soviet states. China's entry into the WTO in 2001 marked a transformation in its global trade relations and accelerated its economic growth.

At the UN Security Council, the newfound spirit of cooperation led to a surge in peacekeeping operations, with a mission expanded to multidimensional peacebuilding and governance support. Twenty-five newly independent countries from the former Soviet Union and Yugoslavia joined the UN between 1990 and 1993. Still, the US remained the unchallenged global superpower. The fast and successful completion of the First Gulf War, with a broad coalition backing the US, emblematized American military and diplomatic might.

By now we know how the next part of the story goes. The US invasion of Iraq without UN Security Council authority in the Second Gulf War was seen widely, including in much of Europe, as a declaration that Washington would exempt itself from its own rules. Charges of double standards grew louder. The overconfident West became distracted by its international blunders and internal struggles, and other nations began looking elsewhere for leadership and partnership.

With hindsight, we can see that the West missed a critical opportunity to consolidate liberal democracy, instead helping to set in motion the multiplication, regionalization, and distrust that explain much of today's fragmentation. By multiplication, I mean an exponential increase in players and fora in international cooperation. By regionalization, I mean a flourishing of countries making economic and military pacts with their neighbors rather than the wider world. Distrust is self-explanatory.

These trends were not all negative, but they were certainly disruptive. And what is more, they led the Global West as traditional guardian of the international order to find itself in a defensive position. Multilateralism began to turn into multipolarity, a structure creaking from latent tensions.

Multiplication
Power today is scattered, kaleidoscope-style, into a dizzying array of ever-changing shapes and combinations. In 1990, the US appeared to command the globe. Now small command centers appear everywhere—which makes it hard to contain countries' diverging interests or connect them to the common good.

The pace of this proliferation first became apparent in the early 1990s. International organizations, actors, and fora multiplied. New interactions between East and West mushroomed as the weight of the Iron Curtain lifted. The internet and affordable air travel made cross-border coordination easier. The *Yearbook of International Organizations* reports that the world's non-governmental organizations grew from about 16,000 in 1990 to over 26,000 in 2017.

The leadership vacuum wasn't the only thing driving this multiplication. There were proliferating global issues in which many actors had a stake and wanted a say. Migration, trafficking, international crime, communicable disease, intellectual property, and environmental crises grew more acute and demanded joint solutions. At the same time, nations grew increasingly aware of the distribution of "global public goods," including climate stability, water, natural resources, cultural heritage, health, and more. Actors from businesses to civil society, science to arts, and activism to sub-national governments started to stake their claim to share in global governance of critical issues.

Meanwhile, the spaces where states met changed. Informal groupings became important alternatives to formal organizations. From the G7, a set of large Western economies that discuss economic policy, grew the more inclusive G20, including nineteen of the world's biggest economies plus the EU, and nowadays the African Union.

And then there were more: The Middle East Quartet to support Middle East peace. The African Union, established in 2002 to promote cooperation on the continent. BRICS, including Brazil, Russia, India, China, and South Africa, since expanded to include ten countries. The emerging BRICS economies combine 40 percent of the world population, 30 percent of world land surface, 24 percent of global GDP, and 18 percent of trade in goods. And they have, in a relatively short time, become a serious competitor to the Western-dominated G7.

These kinds of informal organizations, or "clubs," tend to be smaller than formal multilateral institutions, more issue-oriented, and have fewer rules. Governments appreciate that they are less binding and more confidential, with fewer strings attached. Yet they wield considerable power.

Eastern powers, including China and Russia, like to promote multipolarity with the argument that it frees other nations from Western dominance. (Many of their neighbors, however, fear that Beijing and Moscow seek to replace Western power with their own.) My counterargument is simply to look at what a multipolar world without regard for common rules leads to: chaos, disorder, and conflict. The sustainable solution is not fragmentation, it's fairness.

Regionalization

As international groups became more numerous, they also became more localized. From the smaller number of global-scale efforts that followed World War II, the world spun into many arrangements in each corner of the globe. It was as if the neighborhood association split into a dizzying array of permutations organized by bloc—a clear sign that the neighbors were hungry for change.

The EU may be the most successful example of regional integration, but it is far from the only one. Major organizations exist on all continents. Almost eighty have emerged since 1945. Many of them emphasize economic cooperation—the realm where countries expect most benefits from common rules. They include, for example, the Association of Southeast Asian Nations (ASEAN), Latin America's Andean Pact (AP) and the Economic Community of West African States (ECOWAS), all created in the 1960s and 1970s.

The pace of regionalization accelerated starting around 1990. Prominent new entrants included the Mercado Común del Sur (Mercosur) in South America, the North American Free Trade Area (NAFTA), and the Asia-Pacific Economic Cooperation (APEC). Regional organizations also widened their scope, stretching beyond economics to assert geopolitical influence where member interests aligned.

The agreement to pool sovereignty, of course, does not guarantee smooth cooperation. Lose-lose is in a constant tug-of-war with win-win. Yet despite these challenges, regional organizations have become ever more openly a tool of geopolitics, often with the largest regional powers in the lead. China is an especially assertive player. It leverages its economic power and its global infrastructure project, the Belt and Road Initiative, to incentivize regional cooperation, casting itself as lead partner.

The emergence of such groups in one region of the world naturally inspires competitors in others. Russia has tried (without much success) to drive economic growth through the Eurasian Economic Union (EAEU), a common market of former Soviet states. The Shanghai Cooperation Organization (SCO), in contrast, has realized more gains and holds the potential to become a heavyweight in a future global balance of power. The group, which has a formal charter and a permanent secretariat in Beijing, includes China, Kazakhstan, Iran, Belarus, Kyrgyzstan, Russia, Tajikistan, Uzbekistan, India, and Pakistan. SCO members make up almost a quarter of the world's GDP, and its cooperation covers trade, military affairs, and politics.

The Global West, too, has reacted to this new regionalism. The US has intensified security cooperation in the Indo-Pacific by reviving the Quad (with Australia, India, and Japan), establishing AUKUS (Australia, the United Kingdom, and the US), and sharing intelligence with the "Five Eyes" nations, including AUKUS plus New Zealand and Canada.

The EU, for its part, vigorously promotes EU-Africa partnership and has created its own infrastructure program, Global Gateway, to counter Chinese regional advances. A G7 effort, the Partnership for Global Infrastructure and Investment, also invests to improve health care, telecommunications, and energy in the developing world but explicitly promotes democratic values.

None of these agreements constitute true alliances (and some have already started to wane). They are purpose-based groups, primarily economic. Yet there is no denying that big economic dependencies tend to engender political alignments.

The net effect of all these new fora is not necessarily bad for a rules-based, multilateral order. But it does demonstrate that the current order no longer meets participating states' expectations. On many levels, these are healthy signs of greater participation by more societies in international politics, and an acknowledgment that regional cooperation carries greater benefits than regional rivalry. In fact, regionalization could serve as a good first step to building stronger, more balanced multilateralism—depending on how it is used. These groups not only have an interest in promoting regional peace and prosperity but also tend to know the players and the playing field.

The difference between healthy and unhealthy regionalism lies in how these arrangements are structured and whether they are purely transactional or more systemically cooperative. For regionalism to support a multilateral world order, it must feed into a larger system based on shared values. It must be part of something bigger.

Nations can only do that effectively, however, if we trust each other.

Distrust

The boom in economic cooperation after the Cold War has paid global dividends. Global GDP more than quadrupled between 1990 and 2022. Global trade grew six times over the same period. By 2015, UN data show that more than a billion people had risen out of extreme poverty. Emerging markets such as India, Brazil, Indonesia, and above all China, were among the winners of globalization throughout the 1990s.

That rosy picture, however, is not what it really feels like in many states, especially in the Global South. When I speak with leaders there, they tell me their countries bear an unduly high share of the world's burdens and receive an unduly low share of the benefits. Climate change, for example, affects Sudan and its neighbors much more profoundly than Finland. Many Western nations have fueled their economic growth on four pollution-generating industrial revolutions, but now that climate change is upon us, we tell developing nations they cannot do the same. The global currency transfer system is based on dollars. Yet when migrants try to move to the West for economic opportunity, we tell their countries to keep their people home.

In this context, multipolarity both reflects and accelerates the third global trend: a loss of trust in the multilateral system. This lost trust is probably the most significant factor in the slow decline of the liberal world order—and the most difficult to overcome.

To cross this chasm we must understand its causes. I contend that it essentially springs from three sources: disillusionment, lack of representation, and general populism. We need to rectify all three.

Disillusionment has as much to do with perception as reality—but both perception and reality depend on where you sit. Growth was distributed evenly in recent decades, but economic inequality rose in parallel across the globe. The long-term impacts of COVID, inflation, and food supply challenges from the war in Ukraine dampened development prospects further. The world's richest 1 percent now own about half the world's wealth. The lesson is that "economic growth" remains a relative term.

These trends provide the ferment for growing disillusionment toward an international order associated with Western leadership. The discontents are not confined to poorer nations in the Global South. Even in the world's richest nations, many feel the spoils from technological advances and globalization have been grabbed by the richest people. The working classes have been left behind.

Many of the Global South's grievances are also justifiably linked to their lack of agency in the global architecture. Brazil and India (along with Germany and Japan), for example, have long campaigned for inclusion as permanent Security Council members. So have the UN's African group and the African Union.

That's not to say there has been no progress. The appointment of Nigerian Finance Minister Ngozi Okonjo-Iweala as WTO director-general recognized Africa's importance in the global economy. The World Bank and IMF, however, remain firmly under Western control. An informal agreement assures that the US chooses the World Bank president and Europe the IMF managing director. IMF voting rights are linked to the size of each member state's economy. Consequently, the US holds about 16 percent of the votes, almost as many as the next three (Japan, China, and Germany) combined. World Bank decision-making reflects similar quotas.

There may be good reasons to connect voting rights to member states' economic investments, but this does not erase the impression among states on the receiving end that others decide their fate.

The third source of international distrust is the most global. Whereas disillusionment and unequal representation are felt most keenly by the Global South, populism fuels distrust across societies. The populist narrative, simply put, holds that international cooperation robs you of sovereignty, and lost sovereignty strips your national interests. In other words: globalization has benefited only a few.

Early signs of a backlash against globalization appeared in protests against G8 meetings and the memorable 1999 Seattle riots against the WTO. In 2005, both French and Dutch voters rejected the proposed European Constitution as a crowning jewel in European integration. This marked the limits of popular support for losing more national sovereignty into a cloud of multilateralism.

A common trope in populist discourse, left or right, is to blame domestic challenges on international entanglements. Right-wing populists like Italy's Matteo Salvini and France's Marine Le Pen bash liberal migration policies. Donald Trump built or replaced more than 400 miles of wall on the Mexican border in his first administration, then launched his second with a wave of deportations. Left-wing populists, for their part, attack trade agreements for watering down labor, health, and environmental standards. Many European voters rejected a transatlantic trade agreement, TTIP, over similar concerns.

The phenomenon is not limited to the West. Populist leaders across the globe fashion themselves as an alternative to the supposed elitism of liberal democracy, both domestic and international. In his first UN speech, Brazil's far-right president Jair Bolsonaro lectured the General Assembly: "We are not here to erase nationalities and sovereignties in the name of an abstract global interest. This is not the global interests organization." Similar rhetoric is rising in nations such as Turkey, India, Slovakia, and Hungary. When people fear that their share of the pie is shrinking, they want to keep the whole dish within their control.

Conclusion
"It is true that economic globalization has created new problems. But this is no justification to write off economic globalization altogether. Rather we should adapt to and guide globalization, cushion its negative impact, and deliver its benefits to all countries and all nations."

This could have been said by the head of any G7 government, the president of the European Commission or the trade minister of any Western nation. But it was said by Chinese President Xi Jinping attending in person, for the first and only time, the World Economic Forum in Davos in 2017.

Xi gave the speech days before the first inauguration of Donald Trump. Here was the chairman of the world's biggest communist party appearing as a champion of free trade and an open international order. The message rang loud and clear: If the West steps down from leadership, China is ready to step in. In reality, Beijing has adeptly supported those parts of the multilateral order from which it profits—notably trade—while repudiating those that confine it, such as international tribunal rulings against its maritime expansionism in the South China Sea.

Six years later, Davos 2023 was titled "Cooperation in a Fragmented World." Its very name captured that international governance was in flux. UN Secretary-General António Guterres spoke of a "perfect storm" and called the Davos audience to action, saying: "It's time to forge the pathways to cooperation in our fragmented world."

The good news, and I mean this sincerely, is that we have come to recognize the chaotic state of multilateralism today. And within that chaos we can find the elemental materials for building something new.

For example, today more states and non-state actors than ever are engaged in some form of international cooperation (albeit not always on equal terms). In a complex world with complex problems, we have developed a complex web of tools to tackle them. The results are not always satisfying, and the procedures lack transparency, but as evidenced by the Paris Climate Accords, the system can still deliver. This recognition should not lead us to dismiss multilateralism as defunct or inefficient, but to ask the right questions about it: What do we need to change to improve its workings? Which parts work well and should be kept? How can we reimagine what doesn't?

All relationships, whether between people or nations, are built on trust. And trust, once broken, is difficult and time-consuming to rebuild. But it can be done. Look, for example, at Germany and France, who less than a century ago were riven by military occupation and genocide, whose citizens still hold memories of loved ones killed by the other nation, and who now work across politics, economics, and security as close international partners.

The truth is that this crisis has unequivocally strengthened my belief in multilateralism. Now more than ever, facing global-scale challenges, I believe that nation-states' behavior must be contained and channeled through multilateral institutions. The question is how and in which institutions. People say that if the UN didn't exist, we'd have to invent it. We should refocus on the matter of how to *reinvent* it. And do so, at last, with everyone from the Global West, East, and South at the table.

Part Two
Balance

The Global West

June 2016. Grundsö in Barösund, a rugged island in the Finnish archipelago. Across two seas, the citizens of Great Britain are voting on whether to remain in the European Union.

I watch five-meter flames leap from our bonfire and finally flicker beneath the midnight sun, celebrating Finland's midsummer holiday. I go to bed confident that Brexit won't happen.

I glance at my phone around 3:00 a.m. Brexit! This was not supposed to be possible. Has the UK lost its senses?

Three weeks later, London, a BBC town hall debate. More than a thousand people pack the theater. A fellow panelist wonders why voters abandoned the benefits membership has brought to the UK, including exponential GDP growth. An audience member stands and shouts: "Yeah, perhaps your GDP, mate, but not mine!" The audience applauds.

I realize my view on the EU is naïve. From where I sat in London, Brussels, Luxembourg, Florence, or Helsinki, I believed the benefits of European integration (and global multilateralism) were obvious to everyone. I was wrong.

Fast-forward five months, and American voters elect Donald Trump to his first term as president—another undeniable sign that voters on both sides of the ocean are unsatisfied with the status quo. It looks increasingly like democracy in its current form is not always delivering the essential goods (security, education, health care, equality, opportunity) that people across the globe expect.

But just because democracy does not produce the results you want does not mean it has failed—probably the opposite. It is a system made to change. And if it drifts off course, democracy, unlike authoritarianism, has a self-correction mechanism. We need to learn to apply it better.

By many measures, the Global West seems like the natural heavy hitter on the world stage. It has been the most dominant force in politics, economics, and technology for two centuries. Democracy has its roots in Western political thought. Capitalism and communism both spring from Western economic theory and practice. The first, second, third, and now fourth industrial revolutions drove growth and prosperity in the West before spreading to other corners of the world.

The Global West also encompasses roughly a quarter of the world's nation-states, accounts for around 60 percent of total global GDP, and is home to 15 percent of the global population. The glue that holds these countries together is a mix of shared history and common values, geographic proximity, and broadly aligning interests. The bond manifests in informal and formal alliances in fields like trade and security, plus a multitude of cultural and social exchanges.

Internally, the Global West has created growth, prosperity, and welfare through a combination of political and economic freedom. Most of its political systems converge on democracy (some more liberal, others less) and capitalism (some more regulated, others less). Greece can claim to have laid the foundations for ancient democracy. The United States and France can debate which was the first modern democracy. Finland and New Zealand can battle for status as the first to have real universal suffrage. These open societies provide opportunities, albeit not always equally to all, and allow individuals to live as they see fit, provided they follow commonly agreed laws.

Reality, however, has not always measured up to aspirations. Many other states correctly point out that the West has a history of breaking the global rules it promotes. It has used its economic and technological advantage to conquer, rule, and exploit other regions and peoples. Western powers have not been alone in pursuing imperial ambitions, but they have spoken most loudly against them.

The twentieth century was also marred by two world wars, caused by Europe. The West did learn its lessons and drove the establishment of an international system that avoided another global military conflict for decades.

The legacy of this history for the Global West is mixed. The international system fashioned by the West laid the groundwork for development cooperation and economic progress to reach most regions of the world. It did not, however, eliminate colonialism at once, nor did it prevent bloody regional conflicts. And the system's central challenge remains: to reduce economic and political imbalances within the global constituency it claims to serve.

All of which places the Global West at a watershed. It has all the necessary elements to play a powerful role in crafting a new world order. It has resilient political systems, a strong economic model, and a technological advantage in many key fields. Yet the coming years will determine whether those assets translate into meaningful global leadership—the outcomes depending in significant part on how the West builds on its strengths and contends with its weaknesses to meet this moment.

Politics—Democracy Is Messy but Necessary
The critical questions for all three global spheres—West, East, and South—cut across politics, economics, technology, and geopolitics. I'll take these in turn, politics first.

Democracy is inherently messy. As a president and former prime minister, I know this personally.

Democratic leaders inevitably find themselves moving from one crisis to another. Dissent is constant. Compromise is critical yet cumbersome. New communication technologies have only accentuated this truth. Yet what makes democracy messy—the mission for a diverse people to govern itself through open consideration of different viewpoints—is also what makes it essential. The combination of democracy, equal opportunity, and freedom forms the bedrock of countries that top global rankings from happiness to quality of life, economic stability to GDP per capita, safety to security, and education to equality. This is no coincidence.

I remain unshaken in the view that democracy, even with its imperfections, is far and away the best form of government on earth. Yet as the world wrestles to define its shared future, we must also recognize the ways in which democracy today represents both an asset and a challenge—and get serious about strengthening it.

Among the big questions democracies must answer is how to update their political and economic models as technology becomes the main instrument driving both. Will technology and social media benefit democracies or dictatorships? How do we reap the benefits of instant communication while containing the risks? Will the Global West remain a united force for change or sink deeper into polarization?

These challenges are exacerbated by the rise of populism in nations across the Global West. Many populist leaders, right and left, do not have answers to the grievances they raise. But they do speak to a genuine problem. Many voters see the system as tilted against the majority in favor of global elites.

A brief look at the state of Western democracies will help us assess how ready they are to meet these challenges—and what steps are needed to strengthen them.

The essential frame for the legitimacy of democratic systems is respect for the rule of law. Most Global West countries have strong democratic institutions and a separation of powers between the legislative, executive, and judiciary. This does not mean such institutions are immune to challenges and attacks. But significant challenges are usually less conspicuous than military coups or violent mobs. Take, for example, the ways we communicate.

In today's real-time news cycle, decision-makers are expected to react to events as they unfold. The plethora of views, supercharged by opinions masquerading as news, makes compromise more difficult. Populism and disinformation fuel a constant demand for change. There is little time for reflection or nuanced positions. As a result, short-term thinking takes precedence over long-term. Stopgap solutions bank on the arrival of the next crisis to shift public focus. When any thoughtful statement is immediately overwhelmed by an onslaught of online attacks, many moderate thinkers retreat from the debate and we end up with decision-making by the loudest, not by the silent majority. This is an existential challenge for democracy.

Deeper challenges also confront Western politics. The victories of President Trump or the Brexiteers reveal profound underlying tensions and social problems within the West's democracies. In the US, the two-party system, Republicans versus Democrats, has paired with 24/7 media and other forces to nurture an increasingly toxic political climate. The United States of America is becoming the divided society of America.

At the root of this tension are socioeconomics. Rising economic inequality, fierce employment competition, and the disruptive impact of technology and globalization, especially in labor-intensive industries, have fostered economic and social stagnation. While the rich reaped the rewards of free trade and technological advance, the incomes of blue-collar workers plateaued. White-collar workers see their economic security threatened by artificial intelligence. Our kids, many voters say to themselves, will not live a better life than we did. This economic squeeze, paired with declining birthrates and increasing immigration, has triggered deep cultural anxieties. Many of the countries that preach equal opportunity do not feel equal to those who live in them.

The structures in place to meet these challenges vary from country to country. The Swiss model—frequent voting on current issues—is lauded by those who urge more direct democracy. Some, like Finland, have coalition governments and prime ministers as chief executives. Others are run by presidents.

The European Union is, of course, not itself a democracy—as those who disagree with supranational representation point out. But it is a union of twenty-seven democracies that have decided to pool sovereignty in certain areas for mutual benefit. Its contract describes it as a political union bound by shared values, including democracy, equality, the rule of law, and human rights. Driven by a common currency and the free movement of goods, services, people, and money, the EU has exclusive competence in trade, competition, customs, and monetary policy. EU law stands above national law. The principle of subsidiarity, however, ensures that the EU takes action only where national or local action would be less effective.

At the same time the European Union is a regulatory superpower. When the EU regulates, the rest of the world follows, most of the time. With nearly 450 million consumers, the EU common market is the biggest open single market in the world. Its standards in antitrust, environmental protection, data privacy, services, commerce, health, and safety, to name a few, force multinational corporations to follow. This soft power—or the "Brussels Effect," as Anu Bradford has called it—has been a key element in the EU's success.

The values the EU claims to promote, however, can collide with national practices. The European Commission has confronted infringements of the rule of law in Poland (until the 2024 elections) and Hungary. Far-right parties have gained ground in Germany, France, and Italy by promising to curtail interference from Brussels and crack down on immigration. Extreme left-wing parties in Europe, such as the radical Greek Syriza movement, have equally shown their resistance to Brussels.

But—maybe—this is just a sign of messy yet healthy democracy. The critics are free to suggest alternatives, and the dominant parties must prove their programs against opposition.

Western governments have indeed started a pushback to protect domestic rule of law and promote international democracy. Initiatives like US President Biden's "Summit for Democracy," or "D10" (basically an expansion of G7 to include Australia, India, and South Korea), signaled a spirit of resilience. The EU has developed its own mechanisms to identify and prevent rule-of-law problems and react to them when necessary.

For the Global West to stay on top of the game it will have to begin by making sure its own house is in order—proving to itself and the world that democracy is still the most successful model of governance. That democracy delivers what it promises: freedom, equal opportunity, and justice. This means retooling public systems to narrow the widening income gap and provide citizens with the real prospect of economic stability in exchange for hard work; affordable and accessible health care, housing, and retirement; and equal protection under the law. In essence, to make the walk match the talk of democracy. Globally, this also means the West making greater contributions to leveling the world's political and economic playing field.

The process matters as much as the outcomes. I believe that democracies around the world are struggling now because they haven't upgraded to the age of technology. Democracy was designed by philosophers like Locke, Rousseau, and Hobbes in the eighteenth century when decision-making was slow and sought compromise. Now information flows so quickly that we must react quickly. Whereas leaders then had three months to respond to a new issue, now we have about thirty seconds. Sound solutions require far more time for reflection—and can emerge only if we adapt democracy through new policies and mechanisms to slow decision-making down.

As Joe Biden said at the first Summit for Democracy in 2021: "Democracy doesn't happen by accident. We have to renew it with each generation." Renewal means action at all levels: citizens and civil society, companies and community organizations, state and national lawmakers. It can mean finding new modes of citizen engagement, reenergizing local politics, creating digital spaces that foster democracy, and increasing government transparency. If renewal has been a constant feature of Western democracy, it is time to engage in it now.

Economics—Imperfect Capitalism
The Global West is undeniably the world's economic heavyweight, and capitalism, even with its imperfections, has a lot to do with that.

Measured by its share of global GDP, the Global West represents over half of the world's economy. The US and EU form the largest bilateral trade and investment bloc, accounting for about one-third of global trade. The West's economic model is based—at least in theory—on capitalism, free markets, entrepreneurship, free trade, and open competition. Economic growth has enabled most Global West countries to establish what we in Europe would call functioning welfare states. (In the US, where "welfare" has become something of a dirty word, you might call it a social safety net, or the basic education, health care, retirement, and unemployment benefits on which public well-being depends.) That said, the level of the welfare state varies across the Global West. The Nordic countries present probably the most successful model combining capitalism and strong social security networks. The strongest economy and weakest welfare system are found in the United States.

What lessons does this history hold about the Global West's economic position? As always, it's complicated.

Ask people to name the opposite of capitalism, and many will say communism: free markets versus state control. The West's economic power—as well as the East's proclivity for political repression—have only made that contrast appear starker. Yet as world power shifts, we must recognize that the market/state dichotomy is overplayed. All functioning systems reflect a mix between market forces and state regulations. Markets foster innovation, while states provide needed protection. History has demonstrated that fully unregulated markets and fully planned state economies both backfire. The economies that thrive in the future world order will be those that find a healthy balance between the two.

This reality has taken time to become clear. When the Cold War ended, the prevailing economic excitement was all about markets. Many world leaders saw states as an impediment to growth. The collapse of the Soviet economy proved the point. Over the last twenty years, however, the picture has become muddier. A decade of crisis beginning with the Lehman Brothers collapse in 2008 revealed deep cracks in the Global West's economic model. As this Western-generated crisis sparked a sharp global recession, critics around the world saw the drive for ever higher profits as a root cause. The mantra of "market market market" changed to "state state state." The global pendulum started to swing from open toward controlled, from liberalization toward protection.

This shift deepened in 2009, when the eurozone slid into the sovereign debt crisis and several European countries came close to default. Just as democracy is built on personal freedom, capitalism is built on economic freedom. Both systems are full of tensions and prone to crises. The euro crisis put European solidarity to a dire test.

As Finnish finance minister, I saw up close the ferocity of divisions it ignited. Among all the negotiations I've held in government, nothing matched the existential fights over the future of the common currency. It was one of those crises that, rightly or wrongly, split down the line of geographic identity, North versus South. Germany had reluctantly accepted the euro in exchange for price stability and strict currency management. When the rules were broken and the whole eurozone suffered, fiscally rigid Northern countries refused to foot the bill for mistakes made in the South. Yet if we left Greece unsupported its spiral could compromise the euro and the very viability of pooled sovereignty. Negotiations even drove us to ultimatums. In the end we got a deal, and the euro survived—and eventually the crisis led to deeper ties and closer economic coordination within the EU.

While Europe's growth returned slowly, the Chinese economy bounced back much faster. In 2010, it recorded double-digit growth. Introducing the largest domestic stimulus package worldwide, China played no small role in pulling the global economy out of recession. As the decade rumbled on, the Global West fell deeper into the trap of tariffs and protectionism—a tit-for-tat process that ultimately drives economies toward the lowest common denominator—and has only continued to do so. When COVID-19 and, finally, the war in Ukraine disrupted global value chains, many countries began forging strategic autonomy in key industrial sectors. The market liberalization of the early post—Cold War era was over. Protectionism and intervention resurged. In short, the state was back. At least for now.

In the years ahead, all kinds of economic systems, from capitalism to communism, will have to contend with new challenges spurred by technology and the changing nature of work. We have little understanding of what the job market will look like in 2050. As humans cooperate with machines to drive efficiency, many of today's jobs, blue or white collar, will cease to exist.

Economic systems alone cannot solve the resulting problems. Capitalism has been good at driving growth, but politics has been poor at distributing that growth. Yet the purpose of capitalism is ultimately the creation of jobs and welfare. The real value of economic growth is measured in quality of life. Models to achieve this must adapt as life expectancy increases, the gig economy rises, and retirement retreats. No nation state, whether democracy or autocracy, will survive without an effective welfare system. Economic power hinges not only on growth but on the political capacity to support a decent life.

To keep its position, the Global West will have to prove it can deliver both growth and welfare. This means it will have to stay true to its economic model, combining free-market capitalism, competition, and free trade. Deviation from that model—through protectionism, state aid, or anti-competitive behavior—will cost the Global West credibility in the eyes of the world. Or worse, it will cause the Global West to fall behind economic developments in the Global East and Global South.

The balancing act the West faces is to integrate the most beneficial parts of state regulation into a free-market system to deliver the equality and quality of life that it proclaims to preserve. The difficulty is the collision in many voters' minds between the free trade that promotes growth and the social equity that ensures the fruits of growth are widely shared.

The world is watching, but it's not waiting.

Technology—A Fading Edge

Technology is probably the single most disruptive factor shaping the new world order. Artificial intelligence, robotization, the Internet of Things, quantum computing, and biotechnology all have evolving effects that we struggle to grasp. Technology is changing economics and the way we work, politics and the way we communicate, the military and the way we wage war, science, and eventually our nature as human beings. The way we manage this change will be a key factor in the balance of power between the Global West, Global East, and Global South. And for the record, this paragraph was written through dictation into my iPad, not by ChatGPT.

The Global West held the upper hand in technological development for decades. Japan dominated electronics in the 1980s, with companies like Fujitsu, Sony, Toshiba, and Panasonic. Europe, specifically the Nordics, led telecommunications in the 1990s, with Nokia and Ericsson driving the first wave of mobile phones. The US rose in the 2000s, as tech giants such as Microsoft, Apple, IBM, Intel, Dell, Google, Amazon, and Facebook appeared initially as liberators of society, empowering people through digital tools.

Now technology, once a great strength, no longer gives the same edge to Western states. Other nations have caught up. Neither does the West still benefit from tech giants' social status, which dipped as big tech's risks became apparent and big data began to encroach on individual freedom and self-determination. The questions for the Global West are critical: How can technology be used to improve rather than undermine public discourse and democracy? How can it increase efficiency without exacerbating inequality? And how can we ensure that it is used for peaceful ends? The West's continued leadership will hinge on how traditional democracies adapt to ongoing technological disruption.

Some of the West's advantage certainly remains. The European Union, for example, has a strong tradition in research and development, as well as leading infrastructure companies. As a regulatory superpower the EU can nudge global tech companies on privacy, data protection, and antitrust. The EU also has a chance to lead on defining parameters for responsible, human-centric artificial intelligence. But it needs to make sure not to overburden companies with regulation and curtail their competitiveness. The biggest challenge for the EU is unity. The single market does not translate into collective technological power, as countries and companies prioritize their own interests. This, combined with often cumbersome decision-making processes, puts the EU at a competitive disadvantage.

That said, the greatest challenges posed by technology affect all governments, democratic or autocratic, as the technologies that we invented reinvent us. Facebook, Instagram, and X channel our view of the world. Platforms such as Uber, Amazon, Netflix, and Wolt replace traditional service industries. We spend more time in our home offices. Fintech and cryptocurrencies disrupt financial markets. Currency is not cash anymore. Data is the new gold and oil. Much will depend on how that new oil and gold is used.

Technology has also changed the face of war and the nature of security. Drones herald a new era of unmanned combat systems;

robotized systems on the ground are likely to follow. Instant satellite communication provided by Elon Musk's Starlink system helped Ukraine's military defend itself. Strategists can apply AI to satellite data and open-source information to support fighting. At the same time, technology has taken warfare far beyond the battlefield. Our communication spaces, energy grids, and infrastructure have already been targeted by malign foreign actors. So-called hybrid threats blur the line between peace and war.

Perhaps most astoundingly, the technological revolution is changing science. Over centuries science has cut the risk of humankind's two biggest killers, disease and famine, and helped us live healthier and longer lives. Yet humans have still been "subject to the same physical forces, chemical reactions and natural-selection processes that govern all living beings," according to Yuval Harari. Not so anymore. Humans are transcending biological limits. Bioengineering, bioinformatics, and genetic modification are challenging the laws of nature. Scientists already use lab-grown human organs to study disease. Yet globally, this existential transformation is taking place at a wild frontier under a highly variable set of rules.

A healthy technological future hinges in part on regulation, on scales both national and global. And the states that lead on global consensus-building will also have to demonstrate that they can maximize the best and minimize the worst of technology at home. Success at all scales demands sound policies on ethics and privacy. We must decide, within and across nations, who owns data: the state, a company, or the individual? How should data be used? Where do we set the limits of biotech?

Ultimately, technology is neither positive nor negative. It can be used for good or bad. It can advance democracies as much as dictatorships. It can improve or destroy life. If the West wants to win this game, we have to find a comfortable-enough balance between using data to benefit the whole and protecting the individual. And we have to harness technology to better organize our societies and better protect our democracy—using re-energized democratic processes to do so.

Geopolitics and Geoeconomics

Geopolitically, one challenge precedes all others for the Global West: unity.

The West reflects the diversity of roughly fifty nations across four continents. Key players across these regions share broad goals on politics, economics, and technology. Yet their particular interests and approaches naturally diverge. On the urgent conflicts in Ukraine, Israel, Palestine, and Iran, for example, Western leaders broadly want peace but disagree on how to achieve it.

The good news for the Global West, however, is that we share common values. And alliances based on values are stronger than those based on interests.

Building on that strength to cultivate and maintain cohesion is the first of three major tasks for the West if it seeks to hold sway in future international relations. The question remains open whether this coordination will be concentrated in a few central settings, like G7 and NATO, or dispersed in many splintered fora. Second, the West needs to keep space in its antagonism with Russia and China for de-escalation and differentiated approaches by different Western nations. Last, and maybe most important, the West must meet the challenge from the East by engaging more credibly with the Global South, rendering the benefits of the liberal world order that it preaches more accessible and equitable.

The successful resolution of these challenges is far from a foregone conclusion. To see potential ways to get there, we must consider the current state of play for each realm of the Global West, starting with the US.

Within the Global West, the United States is the *primus inter pares*. It is still a military, political, economic, and technological superpower and the ultimate protector of the rest of the West. Without US backing, the war in Ukraine would most probably have been lost.

The United States has been able to project soft, hard, and smart power for over a century. UN data show it was historically the most attractive immigration destination in the world. Every sixth person in the US was born in another country. The US imprint on global culture and consumption remains unparalleled. Seven of the ten most valuable global brands are American. The US is also the undisputed military superpower. It holds around 750 military bases in 80 countries and accounts for 38 percent of global military spending—more than the next nine countries, including Russia and China, combined.

However, its position of relative strength does not prevent its global role from changing. Donald Trump is the loudest, but not the first, to call for a retreat from the status of global policeman. Three underlying trends in US foreign policy predate him: first, a shift in focus from Europe to the Indo-Pacific; second, a strong belief in "great power competition," in which a small handful of great powers constantly compete for hegemony; and third, a foreign policy agenda that is increasingly a function of domestic politics (with Biden's "foreign policy for the middle class" and Trump's "America first" approaches standing as different examples).

Trump is also not the first to call on allies to take on more of the security burden. The unanswered question is to what extent the administration's rhetoric will be matched by a sustained US withdrawal as guarantor of security, whether in East Asia or Europe.

The simultaneous challenge facing Europe is to take on more of the burden of the continent's security. The traditional EU narrative says that it is an economic giant but a geopolitical dwarf. Reality is naturally more nuanced, but it's true that the EU has focused more on soft and smart, rather than hard, power. Now the EU's geopolitical role has started to change, with fresh efforts to bolster Europe's defense capabilities and its strategic autonomy from the US.

China policy represents another potential collision between the US and European allies. The broad consensus in Washington that China presents the most serious threat to the Global West and must be tightly contained is not universally shared in Europe. European governments talk about constraining rather than containing China—maintaining open trade and cooperation on issues like climate change while seeking to restrain its geopolitical grabs. In the US, Trump's policy has yet to resolve apparent contradictions between taking a tough line against Beijing, particularly on trade and technology, while questioning US commitments to Taiwan's and Japan's security.

What's clear is that the EU will not go down the full path of decoupling (i.e., eliminating all dependence on Chinese products and supply chains), which the US at least rhetorically prefers. In reality, economic interdependence between China and the Global West is so big that it would be difficult to decouple. Instead, de-risking, or reducing the risks of interdependence even while maintaining it, has emerged as common working basis across the Atlantic.

The Global West's strongest moments historically have often been grounded in unity. The alliance rebounded around the attack on Ukraine. The question is whether unity can endure. If it does, the Global West's most critical mission is upholding the central principle of the postwar order: that national borders cannot be changed by military force.

The EU, for its part, increased investment in shared defense with the "EU Strategic Compass," adopted shortly after the Ukraine invasion. Views differ across Europe on the role of an EU defense union, but Putin's action spurred a continent-wide increase in defense spending toward, and sometimes above, the NATO target at the time, 2 percent of GDP. In June 2025, NATO allies more than doubled the target to 5 percent of GDP (including 3.5 percent to defense spending and 1.5 percent to defense-related spending). The task now is to build on that unity and demonstrate to the US that Europe will be a much more active partner in defending the West.

Deepening security cooperation between Europe, the US, and Asia also reflects changing dynamics in the Pacific. Japan, Australia, India, and New Zealand have all joined at least one of a variety of security and intelligence sharing groups with the US and partners such as the UK or Canada. South Korea is not yet part of such formats but during the Ukraine war sided strongly with the West.

These relatively new strategic defense positions by East Asia's Western allies underscore a shifting threat perception in the region, with China increasingly seen as a security risk. Japan's former Prime Minister Fumio Kishida explained metaphorically,

"Ukraine may be the East Asia of tomorrow." Planned investments in new military equipment, including Australia's landmark deal to acquire nuclear-propelled submarines, speak a language of deterrence vis-à-vis regional adversaries. In geopolitical terms, Indo-Pacific partners are drawing closer to the US, just as Europeans are against Russia's aggression.

Conclusion

Taken together, these recent challenges position the Global West at a crossroads. Even the West's far-flung countries agree in their threat assessments, recognizing Russia as an immediate aggressor and China as the more potent long-term competitor. They share goals to maintain a stable international security architecture, protect a rules-based international order, and keep a system of open multilateral trade. This unity of vision brings with it the potential to forge and support a cohesive geopolitical strategy across the West—a global strategy separate from the individual policies that each of its nation-states might pursue.

In this pivotal moment, it may appear to skeptics that democracy is lagging behind as history speeds ahead. As someone who has studied the world and sat eye-to-eye with leaders from myriad countries and cultures, I know there is more to the truth than these appearances. The Global West stands on strong foundations across the big challenges of our time—politics, economy, and technology. The difference today is that we cannot rest on them.

The Global East

November 2009. Helsinki. Chinese Vice President Xi Jinping has requested to meet. I am only a foreign minister. But we already see the beginnings of a post-American world, and Xi knows the EU influences global financial markets and trade.

We get talking about technology. "Why are you so restrictive toward some of the Western internet applications?" I ask.

He smiles and says, "Mr. Stubb, you come from the land of Nokia. We live in a competitive world. Why should we open our markets to American or European products? We might even lose." I realize that Chinese tech protectionism is as much about interests as values.

Fast-forward four years. It's almost midnight. Nyagan, Siberia. I am a tired minister of European affairs and trade. Our delegation is here to inaugurate a Fortum power plant, the biggest ever investment between Finland in Russia. Putin is three hours late, his way of showing who is in charge.

Business done, our delegation takes off around 2:00 a.m. When we stop in Russia to refuel, the airport officials refuse to let us fly on. They claim we lack the necessary documentation. We know they want bribes. I lose my patience and show Lavrov's number on my phone. I am about to press the button to call him when they let us go.

I come home frustrated. I am beginning to realize that my idealism about Russia turning into a normal Western state was wishful thinking. At the same time, I see China developing faster than any country in the world. True to Xi's word, it is as much a partner as a competitor, and at times rival to the Global West.

The truth is that while the West was busy feeling like it was on top of the world, China was slowly, stealthily building its power, forging itself into a global force—far more effectively than recalcitrant Russia. Now China has arrived, and the rest of the world can choose to ignore, resist, or cooperate.

In the Triangle of Power, the Global East is challenging the liberal world order, including its values, rules, and institutions. On its podium of influence stand China, Russia, and Iran, in that order.

Since the Ukraine invasion, North Korea has joined these three nations in what many in the West see as an "axis of aggression." China supports Putin economically and diplomatically. Iran supplies arms and drones to Russia. North Korea has sent troops, artillery, and rockets to the front line in Ukraine. Many other nations support China and Russia, directly or indirectly, in the UN or elsewhere.

What provides the glue among this sphere's roughly twenty-five states? The Global East is less about values, more about interests. Yet these countries' interests differ. Some, like Iran, pursue more regional agendas. Others, like Eritrea, Mali, the Central African Republic, or Congo, are primarily concerned with regime stability. Venezuela, Cuba, and Nicaragua share historic economic links with Russia. North Korea existentially depends on China, Belarus on Russia.

This group varies in geography, demography, economy, politics, technology, history, and culture. And as we will see, China and Russia differ in their approaches to the global order. But they are united in their rejection of the current liberal world order and the hegemony of the Global West, especially of the United States. And most of them are happy to see a multipolar world, led by big powers such as China and Russia, and their spheres of interest.

China's political and economic strength and patient strategy position it far better than Russia to lead the Global East toward a new world order that prioritizes authoritarian power and regional self-interest over Western democracy. The Eastern states broadly feel they have not gotten their due credit, power, or piece of the global pie, and they will make whatever alliances they need to get more of that. China has leaned into a fragmented world of disorder to exemplify that strategy, leveraging flexible interstate cooperation for influence.

The upshot is that, whether the West likes it or not, the Global East is a powerful force that works transactionally with others, and we must understand and dance with their interests if we are to counterbalance their disregard for democracy in the new world order.

Politics—The Efficiency and Inefficiency of Autocracy

Monolithic as the Global East may appear in its authoritarianism, there is great variation within its political systems. Autocracy has in some ways bolstered the strength of most but leaves potential weaknesses in their future. For all its economic power, the Global East faces political challenges to shape the world order to its liking. Let's look first at China.

China is a one-party state. The three pillars of power are the Central People's Government, the Communist Party with its chairman at the top, and the People's Liberation Army.

China is often described as an unusually homogeneous country; over 90 percent of its population is Han. Compare that to the US, a self-described "melting pot," or the EU, composed of twenty-seven diverse states and even more cultures and histories. The Chinese have a strong sense of common culture and civilization. The idea of building walls (not to keep its people in but to keep foreigners out) is enshrined in the national anthem. I once asked George Yeo, former foreign minister of Singapore, the same question that I posed to Vice President Xi in 2009. His answer was revealing: "Alex, China builds walls for everything. Not just physical walls, but also walls for capital flows, cultural imports, foreign movies, educational material, cyberspace, and, as we saw in recent years, bacteria and viruses."

China is historically a mix of law and aspiration to harmony, rather than a strict authoritarian order. The Qin and Han Dynasties unified China over two thousand years ago, standardizing everything from weights and measures to writing. Over four centuries, the dynasties' ruling philosophy developed from legalism to Confucianism, emphasizing rituals and proper behavior rather than strict obedience to law. Confucius talked about cultivating the self, raising the family, and governing effectively. The desired result? A world of harmony, with a grounding in law.

China's zero-COVID policy—criticized by the West—illustrates this combination. If authorities detected cases in a community, they immediately locked it down for weeks or months. Many Chinese people hated the draconian measures, but they complied. The speed of lockdown and level of compliance would not have worked in the Global West, which puts individual freedoms ahead of collective obligation. The point is not whether the policy succeeded, but that it was even possible.

China is also a country of big projects and visions. The now discarded one-child policy and the recurring five-year national economic plan are but two examples of centralized decision-making. Some big projects implemented in the name of the common good have caused immense pain to the population—including the brutally repressive Cultural Revolution. The big visions, combined with economic growth and general welfare improvements, are what maintain relative peace and calm domestically. They also aim to project global power.

Some see the Belt and Road Initiative as colonialism 3.0, a Chinese colonialism, others as a genuine attempt to improve global trade. By the same token "Made in China 2025," Xi's strategy to boost Chinese innovation, can be seen by a cynic as an attempt to steal as much Western intellectual property as possible, rather than to promote genuine global cooperation in technology. And perhaps, for some observers, the "Beautiful China" environmental protection initiative means moving polluting industries to Africa, not improving the continent's economic welfare. Either way, it's clear that China is a power with patience—one which has slowly but surely widened its networks and established closer ties with countries around the world.

In Russia the methods of dominance differ, as does the culture. Russia has long been louder than China in its call to change the world order. In fact, it has been making proposals for a post–Cold War security structure since the mid-1990s. The common denominator of its proposals, which I discussed often with Lavrov during my previous stints in office, was that Russia should sit in the center of that system. I remember seeing draft charters of a new European security order sent from Moscow now and then. They expressed growing antagonism and revisionism in Russian thinking but could not be treated as serious proposals. The reason was simple: they were all about superpower nostalgia, a world that did not exist anymore. Or that is at least what I thought.

More recent history illustrates what the Russian vision is all about: size and power over state sovereignty and international law. This vision has kept Russia reliant on imperialism and natural resources, not innovation, and contributed to its stagnation.

To understand why, consider that Russia has been an authoritarian and imperial state for centuries, and it becomes frustrated when its powerful self-image does not match geopolitical realities. The system of governance has always centered around a supreme leader, be it a tsar, party leader, or president. The leader derived his or her rights from God (tsar), the class struggle (party leader), or general societal stability (Putin). Romanov dynasty rulers pursued modernization and imperial conquest to establish Russia as a successful, ambitious, and glorious power by the late eighteenth century. This image remains deeply ingrained in Russian self-understanding today.

The empire ultimately expanded from the Baltic and Black Seas all the way to Alaska and the Pacific, becoming the third largest empire in world history. However, as Europe industrialized and other societies adapted to new economic realities, reforms in Russia began to fall behind. Under pressure from a growing workers' class, the still largely feudal society began to crack. The traumatic military defeat in World War I was final evidence that the

Russian Empire had not kept up with history. Russia plunged into revolution and a civil war that lasted five years. The Bolshevik Party, led by Vladimir Lenin, finally established its power, and the Soviet Union arose from the blood-drenched soil of the former empire.

In terms of economic, technological, and political strength, the Soviet era marks arguably Russia's high point in history. At incredible human costs, Soviet leader Joseph Stalin forced industrialization through the Union's vast territory. Russia, with the other Allied powers, defeated Nazi Germany and remained the only global military power next to the US after 1945. It developed its own atomic bombs and nuclear energy. It sent the Sputnik satellite and the first man into space. But a few decades on, the system—this time communism—again proved incapable of keeping up with global change.

This eventful, if abbreviated, Russian history is important to bear in mind. Its narratives determine much of the way Russians think about themselves and their neighbors and enemies today. Stability is associated with Russian greatness, expansion, progress, and cultural richness. Chaos signals trouble.

But underlying tensions between poor segments of society and a thin ruling elite—which haunted tsarist Russia—remain fundamentally unresolved. Russia today is a poorly organized, inefficient, and essentially corrupt petrostate that derives between 30 to 50 percent of its public budget from oil and gas exports. The close-knit elite keep their positions only through loyalty to the present leader. Perhaps this system confers short-term strength, but it is a long-term weakness.

These conditions explain why Russia's recent development has been the inverse of China's. Military spending stagnated during the 1990s. The Russian population shrank from 148 million in 1990 to 144 million today and is expected to fall further. Its per capita GDP only returned to its 1990 level in 2004. The dismantling of the Soviet Union into fifteen independent states was a geopolitical tipping point. Russia never got over it, and much of its rogue behavior in former Soviet territory is linked to its superpower nostalgia.

The Russian and Chinese autocracies enjoy stability—for now—because from the inside they appear to provide order and, at least in China, economic progress. Their power is also underwritten by tight control over the media and information, allowing them to present self-promoting narratives and block diverging ones. To some outside actors they are attractive partners, offering cooperation without asking difficult questions about human rights or good governance. Yet it is worth remembering that authoritarianism renders not only human rights but also stability and even success fragile. Authoritarian regimes seem to be tolerated from the inside only as long as there is either continuous economic growth or relentless control. If one or both evaporates, collapse is only a question of time.

Turning the lens to the rest of the Global East, we see an array of countries that don't fit a single mold. But they converge on two characteristics: political freedom is close to nonexistent, and poverty is widespread. All of Russia's core supporters other than China are dictatorships of various shades: Belarus, Iran, North Korea, Syria (under Assad), Eritrea, Nicaragua, and Mali. Others that took a more moderate pro-Russian stand at the UN after the Ukraine invasion, including Cuba, the Central African Republic, Laos, and Vietnam, offer little more freedom. Only the Bahamas and Bolivia, which voted at least once in Russia's favor, can be located on the democratic spectrum. Most Global East countries depend heavily on commodity exports and rank low on national income. International development data show that Russia's supporters in the current geopolitical confrontation are a club of very poor autocracies. This does not mean, however, that we should underestimate their influence.

Economics—State and/or Capitalism
Most economies of the Global East can be described as in transition, with an inescapable dependence on trade with the West. Yet they are keen to find alternatives and become less exposed to the West's economic power. Each state's potential ultimately hinges not only on its resources but also on how well its authoritarian government manages to play within international markets—a feat that some are achieving more successfully than others.

Chinese state-driven capitalism, the hub of the Global East's economic spokes, has strengths and weaknesses. Its successful economic opening and subsequent growth have driven immense changes in Chinese society over forty years. Modernization has spread. Poverty has decreased. Both average incomes and income inequality have increased.

China has scale, speed, and drive. The size of its workforce, plus a strong central government with a collective mandate and a capacity to implement policy, gives China a competitive advantage. Its ruthless culture of competition, strong work ethic, and yearning for wealth make it a formidable global contender. Many in the Global West and Global South have observed China's growth rates with envy, some starting to look at the Chinese model for solutions.

The system, however, has its weaknesses. State control combined with bureaucracy rarely leads to innovation. China has a weak currency, excessive debt, limited information flows, and plenty of internal dissonance. The legacy of the one-child policy is a shrinking labor force supporting a growing elderly population. Human rights violations, weak environmental standards, limited welfare, and excessive control could spill into general social unrest and demands for more freedoms.

The only certain thing about China's future governance is that it will have to become more decentralized. Fiscal decentralization has already proven a source of growth. It gave local governments tools and incentives to develop their cities and regions and promoted the emergence of private companies that could raise productivity faster than the state economy. This regional flexibility helped channel a carefully controlled national opening to foreign investment and policies to secure international technology transfers. Many observers contend that infringements of intellectual copyrights—and even business espionage—have also played their role in the Chinese economic miracle.

While China turned strategically and selectively outward during the 1990s, Russia sputtered. In 1990, Russia's GDP still surpassed China's by over 40 percent. Today, China's economy dwarfs Russia's by a factor of ten. The reasons are manifold. Russia entered the 1990s as an exhausted state-run economy. Its economic transition stumbled on haphazard privatization, inflation, corruption, and social hardship. A decade-long recession followed.

Further reforms, and above all rising oil and gas prices, finally stabilized the Russian economy in the early 2000s. Growth returned at moderate rates. Domestic consumption, foreign investment, and economic diversification grew. But challenges remained: in an economy still dominated by large state-owned companies, innovation never took off. Following Russia's illegal occupation of Crimea and Donbas in 2014 and the international sanctions it sparked, Russia's economy lost momentum again. Declining energy prices reduced state revenue. Today, Russia remains an important trading partner for many countries, especially in defense and energy. But as innovation and diversification slow, its economic competitiveness keeps decreasing.

China understands this and, despite the neighbors' deepening trade relations, does not depend on Russia to thrive. Russia is a useful source of raw materials, including oil and gas. Yet for China the West's banks, finance, and business are simply much more important. In 2021, its exports in goods to the US and EU each totaled more than seven times its exports to Russia.

The economies of the remaining Global East countries are similarly transitionary, with some liberalizing more than others. Many, especially in Africa, are starting from a very poor level. Cuba, Laos, and Vietnam maintain a high degree of state planning. North Korea remains the world's most closed economy, except for its trade with Russia. Vietnam has achieved noticeable successes in recent years, whereas Iran and Venezuela have suffered under international sanctions. During my visits as minister for foreign trade I discovered that former Soviet republics in Central Asia were, like Russia, dependent on oil and gas exports, but unlike Russia, working toward modernization.

Looking ahead, the Eastern economies to watch are likely to be those with young and growing populations, sufficient technology infrastructure and connectivity, and critical minerals. China and Russia remain the economic power centers, although each plays in a different league. They will probably continue their efforts in "de-dollarization"—attempting to reduce exposure to Western economic power plays. Some Eastern partners will welcome this. But it is far from clear that this is enough to lure other Global East countries into following their geopolitical lead. For the foreseeable future, economic cooperation within the Global East will remain a tactical choice grounded in short-term political objectives and the presence or absence of viable alternatives.

Technology Decides the Future
In 2016 I wrote a *Financial Times* op-ed with the slightly provocative title: "For China, Europe Is the New Africa." I argued that China was mining European technology, patents, and intellectual property much like Europe mined African natural resources, mostly through thinly veiled state-owned companies. Yet I warned against knee-jerk reactions of protectionism. Soon after the US government intervened in a Chinese purchase of German semiconductor equipment manufacturer Aixtron, whose holdings involved sensitive technology and intellectual property with potential US security implications. The lesson: technology is at the center of both political and economic competition. And for the Global East and especially China, it is the key tool to achieve economic growth and political power.

China's technological ascent after the Cold War may be even more impressive than its economic rise. In the 1990s, China was considered capable of neither large-scale innovation nor offering a domestic market for innovation-based products. World Intellectual Property Organization (WIPO) data shows that in 1996, China filed fewer than 12,000 patent applications while the

US filed over 177,000. Huawei was a small company and mobile phones a luxury afforded only to the party elite.

Twenty years later, China's patent applications surpassed the US by 90 percent, Huawei was the world's biggest telecoms company, and most Chinese owned a smartphone. And this was only the first year of "Made in China 2025." China has since caught up in R&D investment, academic output, and ability to attract international talent, and has gone beyond the catch-up and copying type of innovation. This was partly a play to keep technology under state control, but equally to create national champions. Tencent, Alibaba, and mobile phone brand Xiaomi show that China both produces innovation and provides a vast consumer market. Experts consider China a credible contender for world leadership in future technologies from software design to quantum computing, semiconductors and chips to renewable energy. Militarily, former CIA Director William Burns has stated that technology will be the crux of competition with China and a matter of survival for future US intelligence.

China's centralized steering of industry has fueled its technological rise. The government is willing and able to use limitless resources to catch up to the US. It can also leverage massive troves of state-owned data to gain a competitive advantage. This strength is also a weakness. China's AI investment could ultimately founder on the innovation-suppression of state control. Plus, Chinese innovations often stay local, unlike equivalent US services. Scaling tends to stumble on suspicion about how the Chinese government might use Chinese technology beyond its borders. Limits on information and data flows from the outside world, like blocking Google or ChatGPT, will continue to hold China back.

China is also technologically constrained by the company it keeps. With friends like Finland and Sweden, home to global infrastructure leaders Nokia and Ericsson, the US can leverage its allies' technologies and knowledge for competitive advantage, a luxury China does not have.

China has nonetheless used its innovative power to develop highly sophisticated systems for technological state control. During COVID-19, the government used a vast network of closed-circuit cameras, plus AI, to monitor and control private citizens' every move. Apps such as WeChat gather personal data used to determine everything from mortgages to insurance payments—based on individual credit history, health and exercise habits, nutrition, alcohol consumption, travel, and more. Many Chinese see no problem with that. Most in the Global West would disagree.

Ultimately the tension that all countries face—and that will affect competition between states with differing values—is about data. Every society must decide who should own our data: the state, a private company, or individuals? To prevent concentration of power the only option is to regulate data ownership and control. In a digital dictatorship this regulation is done by the authoritarian state. In a democracy, by us all.

The Russian tech sector, meanwhile, has followed a very different trajectory. The Soviet Union stood for high-quality engineering and innovation in sophisticated fields like aerospace and atomic energy. Post-Soviet Russia remains a foremost exporter of modern weaponry and nuclear-power hardware and expertise. Its growing submarine fleet and the hypersonic Kinzhal missile exemplify its continued military competitiveness.

However, the story of Skolkovo—the Russian Silicon Valley—illustrates the trouble that a Russia on its descent into Putin's autocracy was to encounter. Announced in 2009 by then-President Dmitry Medvedev, the Skolkovo area outside Moscow was designated to house Russia's tech future. The multibillion-dollar investment project aimed to build vast office and lab complexes, welcoming thousands of digital startups, computing firms, and research labs. Microsoft, Samsung, Cisco, and Nokia began to invest; MIT entered a university partnership.

But beyond these flagship participants, large-scale investments did not pour in. Neither did any blockbuster innovation produce a single unicorn startup. Corruption scandals arose and political interference set in. Once in power, President Putin prioritized military modernization, including the development of digital warfare and disinformation capabilities. When Russia invaded Crimea and Donbas in 2014, sanctions put the brakes on Western cooperation. The fast deterioration of civic freedoms kicked off a steady exodus of talent.

The Ukraine invasion then sealed Russia's isolation from Western finance and exchange and reinforced short-term thinking. Resources now sustain an increasingly unsustainable war and plug the holes torn by international sanctions. Massive defense spending diverts investment and workforce from other sectors. Worst of all, hundreds of thousands of young Russians have left the country, adding to an already catastrophic demographic gap. Russia's capacity to drive relevant, marketable innovation is seriously limited. Its dependency on friendly states, above all China, for access to future technologies has deepened.

Beyond Russia and China, innovation and technology are not the strong suit of the Global East, where many countries must battle poverty, fragile statehood, weak governance, and in some cases tight sanctions. Only China, and with great distance Russia and Vietnam, made it into the top 50 of WIPO's global innovation index in 2022. This is despite notable scientific traditions in countries such as Iran. As models, China and Russia appear at opposite ends of the political strong-arming spectrum: While the former used government planning to systematically increase its potential, the latter risks losing what's left of its capacity in an aggressive geopolitical gamble.

Geopolitics

The Global East's shared antipathy to Western dominance presents an opportunity for a large power to leverage that dissatisfaction to assert its influence over the world order. Both Russia and China, of course, aim to do just that. Yet they drive the multipolarity agenda in different ways. As in other realms, China's slow and stealthy strategy is more likely to succeed than Russia's short-term show of force.

A long-standing goal for both Russia and China is to break the bond between the US and Europe. In 1997, they presented a common communiqué under the telling title "Joint Declaration on a Multipolar World and the Establishment of a New International Order." Putin often provocatively speaks of the EU as the vassal of the US. China's approach is more flexible. It distinguishes between the EU and US, attempting to leverage the EU's cooperation to the US's detriment. Yet to the extent that China and Russia collaborate on efforts to splinter the West, their partnership is one of convenience, not values. For China the relationship is utilitarian. For Russia it is existential.

China and Russia are also in the business of trying to split European unity. China's "14+1" (formerly "17+1") cooperation with Eastern and Central Europe intends to create trade and economic links independent from Brussels (albeit slowed by the war in Ukraine). Russia tried preferential treatment for certain European states on energy cooperation, such as the Nord Stream natural gas pipeline to Germany. Russia has also sought to influence public opinion in EU countries through disinformation and propaganda, funding far-right groups and spreading "fake news" during elections.

China's strategy to reshape global relations hinges on positioning itself as a broker and benefactor—and it uses big projects as a geopolitical tool. Take its "Community of Shared Future of Mankind" proposal to reinvent an international order free of the "inherent biases of the existing international order" (hint, hint). Xi's "Global Security Initiative," launched in 2022, spoke in similar code. His underlying message is: China can help as an "equal partner," whereas the West will make cooperation morally conditional. China's pitch is to tweak the West's system to the East's advantage.

In Russia's push for multipolarity it helped formalize the Eurasian Economic Union (EAEU) of several post-Soviet states in 2015, aimed at creating a single market like the EU. However, the economic benefits have neither fueled momentum for further integration nor attracted new applicant states. The Collective Security Treaty Organization (CSTO), founded with similar partners in 1992 as a counterpart to NATO, also has showed meager success, and some members have distanced themselves since the Ukraine invasion. In other ways, the war has provided Russia a forum to push multipolarity further. It deepened security cooperation with China, Iran, and North Korea, forging an alliance Western commentators now call "CRINKs." But China, leveraging flexible alliances, quietly supports Russia's war efforts while also using fora like BRICS or the Shanghai Cooperation Organization to promote alternative visions of cooperation.

In the contest to shape the new world order, China plans for the long-term. It is in no rush to become the global leader. It has all the time, population, and resources to let things happen gradually. "Hide your strength, bide your time," as former leader Deng Xiaoping used to say. And China will. The big question is whether China's governance model is sufficiently adaptable to go all the way. Xi often appears impatient; he pictures himself as a leader destined to steer historic changes, not wait for them to happen.

I have my doubts—at least in the long-term. China will have to orchestrate a gradual opening of its politics, as it has done with its economy. This opening will not lead to traditional democracy, no matter how much the West hopes for it. China will not become a dystopia either. Its model will be a unique combination of state-controlled market capitalism, central planning, more economic decentralization, and digitally enhanced authoritarianism.

The clouds over the Russian system of governance are much darker. It is closer to a renewed period of internal turmoil and economic instability than a renaissance of its role as a global power. Putin is gambling with his remaining national resources and increasingly dependent on his international partners' patience. The gap between the Russian economy and the Global

West will soon be as big as it was when the Soviet Union collapsed in 1991.

Iran, for its part, may be an outlier of the Global East. It is fundamentally a religious state that sees itself as a regional and potentially global heavyweight. Its nuclear ambitions, hostility toward Israel, aggressive meddling in Yemen, and use of proxies to destabilize the region have made it a natural target for US containment. Iran, like Russia, lost position with Assad's ouster from Syria in late 2024. With Iran's proxies (Hamas, Hezbollah, and the Houthis) also severely weakened, Israel and the US saw an opportunity to target the Iranian nuclear program with major attacks. It is still unclear what the long-term impact will be. Given its economic and military potential and its crucial role in the world's most complex geopolitical region, however, Iran remains an important element in the Global East equation. To the West, it remains an awkward unknown.

Conclusion

The Global West's view of the Global East is unified, for the moment, in the belief that Russia's invasion must be stopped and China's global ambitions checked. Internal differences, however, bubble just below the surface and may be amplified by Trump's presidency. The US is much more comfortable than others confronting China. The EU holds a differentiated view of China as "partner, competitor, and systemic rival."

It is, however, the Global South countries, as well as some junior partners of Russia and China, that the Global West needs to take into its geopolitical calculations. Many are driven by economic and developmental needs. They are tired of Western lectures on human rights and of global geopolitical considerations taking precedence over their national concerns. Despite the diversity of their interests, they map onto both Russia's policy of disruption and China's advancement of an alternative world order.

The confrontation between East and West today is different from the Cold War, as our economic and technological (*inter*) dependency is much higher. Ideological competition is also less pronounced. However, the competition is systemic in that it pitches democracy versus autocracy in a race for who can best offer prosperity and security. And the Global South is closely observing who is performing better—and who offers cooperation on better terms.

The Global South

May 2023. I draft a Financial Times *column about the Global South's importance to the new world order and send it to colleagues for comments.*

One response, written by a prominent foreign policy thinker, reads "... my attitude is fuck the Global South.... But, for reasons you will understand, I haven't gotten round to writing that yet. Your piece sounds eminently more rational and publishable."

I know the message is written tongue-in-cheek. But the fact is that it reflects the genuine thinking in many corners of the world. And that thinking is wrong.

It was always a moral mistake to dismiss the Global South as a backwater. But now that the Global South has a critical role to play in the new world order, it is a strategic mistake, too.

The task for leaders across the West and East is to rid ourselves of old-school prejudice and recognize the changes taking place in the Global South. A good starting point is to realize that we live in a world of multiple orders and alliances where the Global South will be the pivotal player, whether we like it or not. And as always, it's better to understand than assume.

The Global South is far from monolithic. But collectively and individually its states have increased their economic heft and political voice. Most see advantage in weakening the old international (they would say Western) order. As the geopolitical calculus changes, Global South nations see an opportunity to leverage their influence and act with a new independence from the West. Nations such as India, Saudi Arabia, Brazil, and South Africa speak with new self-confidence. Many no longer feel a need to call Washington before striking out in a new direction.

The Global South is also receiving more attention than at any time since the 1970s. In that decade of acute Cold War tensions, many countries from Asia, Africa, and Latin America refused to take sides. The group comprised around 90 members (later 120), ranging from Indonesia and India to Yugoslavia, Egypt, Algeria, Ghana, and Jamaica. They called themselves the "Non-Aligned Movement" and demanded new international structures of economics and cooperation. They wanted a voice—agency. But the big powers listened only when it was in their interest. Not much changed.

In fact, when the global economy did change in the late 1970s, it was not the way those countries hoped. IMF and World Bank reforms ushered in a free-market era where competitive advantage rested firmly with developed economies. In 1980, an international commission under former German chancellor Willy Brandt concluded that the world was divided into a rich industrialized North and a poorer developing South. With a few exceptions, countries below the thirtieth parallel had significantly lower economic outputs and standards of living.

Today, development has become a global phenomenon rather than a regional condition. But in politico-economic terms the so-called "Brandt Line" still holds. IMF data show that, not counting China, Russia, and several smaller European states, emerging and developing economies are home to 60 percent of the global population but produce only 28.5 percent of global GDP. Their share of global trade stands at 17.3 percent. This economic disadvantage is one of the defining commonalities within the Global South.

Nonetheless, the Global South is geopolitically resurgent. And within its body politic are many key players, such as India in Asia and Saudi Arabia, Qatar, and the United Arab Emirates in the Middle East and Gulf. In Africa three countries stand for over half the continent's economy: South Africa, Egypt, and Nigeria. Brazil often speaks for Latin America, but Argentina also has the Global West's ear.

Since Russia's invasion of Ukraine, talk of "non-alignment" is back. The leaders of India, Brazil, and South Africa made a point of not openly supporting Russia but not condemning it either. Yet these countries' position is not neutral. They are staking out an agenda of their own. And as someone from the Global West, which has long enjoyed the freedom to pursue its own prerogative, I can understand why. It is easier to claim that values supersede interests if you have agency and economic strength. The opposite holds true if you lack either or both.

India illustrates this approach neatly. Indian Prime Minister Narendra Modi told Putin publicly in September 2022 that today was "not a time for war." Yet India has abstained from all UN resolutions condemning the Russian aggression to date and, as reflected in Bruegel datasets, increased imports from Russia. Former National Security Advisor Shivshankar Menon summed up developing countries' perspective like this: to them, "The war in Ukraine is about the future of Europe, not the future of the world order, and the war has become a distraction from the more pressing global issues of our time."

Whether such diverse nations can stick together is at best questionable. But for now the Global South is leveraging the power vacuum created by East-West upheavals to drive forward its own interests—and insisting that international powers and institutions respect those interests.

Politics—Democracy or Other Priorities
Lumping together more than a hundred countries on four continents, with around 5 billion inhabitants, requires a caveat. These states share interests and aspirations, yet Western preconceptions often miss the subtleties of their diversity. I cannot claim to have studied enough Southeast Asian economy, African history, or Latin American sociology to be an expert on any one region. Then again, not being an expert sometimes makes it easier to see the forest for the trees.

During my years in government, I have visited six continents and met leaders from pretty much every country. It is sometimes my duty to raise issues linked to democracy or human rights, and I feel comfortable doing so, but I always take care to do so in a respectful manner. I try to listen deeply, to understand what matters to my host country before I present Finland's agenda. Every such meeting is an opportunity for learning.

Coming from a smaller country without a colonial past, it is probably easier to have this dialogue. I cannot viably lecture anyone, but I can share the narrative of a country that believed in democracy even when it was poor. Finland, after all, rose from repression and poverty to freedom and prosperity. I have always tried to tell this story without arrogance, only a sense of hope about what can be achieved.

What I have understood through these conversations is that democracy has deep roots in many Global South countries. The sphere includes a spectrum from democracies to autocracies. Many have robust democratic institutions—witness the role of an independent judiciary in Brazil amid political tumult. Others put economic growth and regime stability ahead of democracy. But despite the sphere's democratic inclinations, democracy has not broadly flourished across the Global South. And as its countries grow and assert their global place, democracy may not be their highest priority.

India prides itself on being the world's largest democracy. Its origins lie in the anti-colonial movement of the late nineteenth century. The struggle for independence in the mid-twentieth century was instilled with a strong democratic ethos. Mahatma Gandhi's nonviolent protest embodied a vision of a peaceful and tolerant country that guaranteed civic freedoms. In 1947, the new Constitution declared India a "sovereign socialist secular democratic republic."

Democracy was also a watchword for anti-colonial movements in Africa during the 1950s and 1960s. Under charismatic leaders, Ghana, Kenya, and Senegal overcame colonial rule and established states with democratic foundations. Democracies in Tanzania, Mozambique, Namibia, and Botswana also grew from liberation movements. The people expected democratic institutions to replace colonial administrations. Eventually, South Africa's liberation from apartheid also became a symbol for African democracy. Nelson Mandela's release from prison in 1990, and the negotiated transition from racist authoritarianism to democracy, sent reverberations across the globe.

Democratic idealism, however, did not always translate into facts on the ground. Coups in Uganda, Ghana, and Nigeria ousted civilian governments in the early 1970s. Brutal dictatorial regimes, such as Idi Amin's in Uganda, emerged. More recently, military and authoritarian rule has returned to West Africa, Central Africa, and the Sahel and Horn regions. Reasons range from ethnic and religious tensions to corruption to organized crime and persistent poverty. Worsening climate conditions add to the pressure.

That assessment is not an indictment. International liberals like myself often make two false assumptions about democratic progress. The first is that democracy is somehow a self-evident part of human nature. It is not. On the contrary, democracy tries to contain human nature by a system of mutually agreed laws. The second assumption is that everyone considers democracy the best form of governance. I might believe that, but not everyone does—and certainly not everyone in the Global South. In many places, growth and welfare feel more urgent.

Positive examples also appear in Africa despite war and conflict. Botswana, Cape Verde, and Namibia have proven resilient democracies for decades. In Ghana and South Africa, courts have fought back against leaders seeking to retain power or enrich themselves. Regional organizations like the African Union (AU) and Economic Community of West African States (ECOWAS) have helped stem a democratic rollback.

Forces pressing toward and against democracy also continue to shape regimes in Asia and Latin America. The military takeover of Myanmar contrasts with the overthrow of authoritarian rule through popular protest in Sri Lanka. The Philippines swung away from democracy with the ascent of an authoritarian strongman in 2016, but its new president appears more moderate. Latin America registers a relatively high number of democracies, with autocratic regimes only in El Salvador, Haiti, Honduras, Nicaragua, and Venezuela. How many Westerners know that the small Central American nation of Costa Rica has no military, spends 7 percent of GDP on education, and generates 90 percent of its energy from renewables?

The defense of democratic principles is ongoing business across the Global South. Conditions can change quickly. President Jair Bolsonaro set back democracy in Brazil; current President Luiz Inácio Lula da Silva has made repairs. India held competitive elections in 2024, but Prime Minister Modi has been criticized for discrimination against minorities and suppression of civil liberties.

The Middle East and North Africa were the stage for the biggest drama of democracy in recent decades. Following the self-immolation of street vendor Mohamed Bouazizi in Tunisia in 2010, a wave of protest swept the notoriously autocratic region. Hundreds of thousands of mostly young protesters took to the streets to push back against the economic precarity and unresponsive political systems in which they lived. While regimes fell in Tunisia, Libya, and Egypt, others held on to power, sending police and military to fight back. Syria and Yemen descended into bloody civil wars.

Democracy, however, was ultimately unable to gain a foothold in the region. Bashar al-Assad's cruel regime in Syria did collapse in December 2024, and new President Ahmed al-Sharaa has vowed to uphold peace, respect minorities, and, eventually, hold elections. But if the past has taught us anything, it is to wait and see.

The Arab Spring exemplified the intricacies of political development in the Global South. In many countries, economic stagnation creates unsatisfied popular demands. Entrenched elites, caught in social conservatism, fear losing in the change process and fight back. If we thought social media could create an unstoppable wave of democratic empowerment, Assad's long war on his own population underscored the standing power of brute force. Extremism finds a breeding ground in such violent and fragile environments. What is more, protesting populations do not always aim for democracy.

Adding pressure to the political pot is the large size and young age of Global South populations. Demography may be the second most defining feature distinguishing the Global South, after GDP per capita. Whereas the median age in Europe and North America is around forty, the median age in all other regions is ten years lower. In Africa it drops to nineteen. UN data shows that half the global population increase until 2050 will occur in eight countries: Congo, Egypt, Ethiopia, Nigeria, Tanzania, India, Pakistan, and the Philippines.

These demographic changes hold opportunities and risks, as well as implications for political stability across the Global South. Youth can in some cases be a force for democracy and, as the UN's 2022 World Population Prospects notes, booming populations present economic growth potential, a so-called "demographic dividend." Yet young and growing workforces also raise pressure on governments to provide education and opportunity. If these demands remain unmet, the temperature in these societies will rise and make conflict more likely. Countries under pressure will ask themselves whether democracy or autocracy provides the recipe for success. If they are wise, they might also ask: How can we best unleash the potential of a young, striving generation?

Economics—High Expectations
Economically, the Global South has been on a roll—a fact that explains some of its growing confidence on the international stage. The question for the coming decades, however, will be whether this group can foster the stability and cooperation to sustain their momentum, and whether economic growth will ultimately help to close or widen the gaps within them.

The Global South has been the powerhouse for global economic growth in recent decades. Starting from much lower levels compared to industrialized countries, emerging economies contributed over half the increase in global GDP in the 2010s. UN Conference on Trade and Development data show that trade within the Global South accounts for one-fourth of global trade, and South-South foreign direct investment represents one-third of global FDI.

Asia has seen big economic successes. The "tiger economies" of Hong Kong, Singapore, South Korea, and Taiwan, which took off in the 1960s and 1970s, became emblematic of fast-paced industrialization. Thailand, Malaysia, and Indonesia soon joined them. The 1980s then saw the awakening of the giants: India and especially China, which alone has contributed around 25 percent of global growth in GDP since 1980. These success stories were often the result of state-led industrialization and export orientation. They profited from globalization and a steady increase in global trade—basically their integration into a capitalist global economy.

Beyond Asia, Brazil, Mexico, Argentina, and South Africa also experienced extended periods of growth. In Africa, forty years of catch-up growth since 1980 have produced rising living standards and impressive poverty reduction. But these benefits have been unevenly distributed across the Global South. Most countries in Asia, Africa, and Latin America moved up from low- to middle-income. But only a small minority, such as Chile, Saudi Arabia, or Singapore, moved into the high-income bracket. Little movement occurred among the world's poorest countries, especially in sub-Saharan Africa, where poverty levels remain high and growth prospects meager. The UN list of least-developed countries (LDCs) currently counts forty-six. Since the list's inception in 1971, only six countries have managed to "graduate."

With demographics on their side, emerging markets in the Global South still hold the biggest growth potential within the global economy—but significant obstacles lie in the way.

Despite increases in manufacturing and services, many emerging economies still heavily depend on agriculture and the extraction of raw materials for foreign markets. This is particularly the case in Africa and Latin America. They need investments in infrastructure and access to advanced technology. Deficits in good governance, the rule of law, and human rights create uncertainties that discourage foreign investment. Limited educational opportunities hinder the expansion of human capital. Gender imbalances put girls and women at a systemic disadvantage, especially in parts of Africa, and thus cost these countries an additional source of growth.

It's no help that many of the richest Western nations are turning inward. They talk of decoupling and so-called "friend-shoring," or limiting trade to allies—a move with serious economic implications for the Global South. The IMF finds that foreign direct investment (FDI), an indicator of cross-border economic activity, also has shrunk over the past decade. After years of global integration, we are witnessing the era of economic fragmentation.

The Global South is therefore looking to new sources for development finance. Existing financers, like the IMF and World Bank, have long been criticized for uneven governance structures. Even some regional sources, such as the Asian Development Bank, are Western dominated. Enter the New Development Bank, operating since 2015 and owned almost completely by BRICS, and the Asian Infrastructure Investment Bank, started in 2016 with China as the largest shareholder. Both arise from Chinese initiatives and preside over growing capital resources.

Regional integration is likely to play an important role in boosting economic exchange. Especially in a volatile and fragmented global economy, organizations like MERCOSUR in Latin America, ASEAN in Asia, or ECOWAS in West Africa provide important alternative platforms to coordinate on trade, labor mobility, and investment. South-South cooperation, which was once more aspiration than reality, drastically increased after 1990 and continues to be an economic driver.

It remains to be seen whether intra-South cooperation will lead to a more coherent common agenda to power the Global South on the international stage. Developing countries will have to address internal obstacles to sustainable growth. And their success may hinge on whether great power competition helps or harms prospects for development cooperation.

Technology—Better Than You Think
Kids in Kigali or Kathmandu will know Apple, Google, Samsung, and Huawei. They may have Facebook profiles and sit in internet cafés chatting on IBM computers run with Microsoft's Windows. In the West, what brands from emerging markets (other than China) do we know? There is still a Western perception that associates African technology largely with emails from a Nigerian prince offering a commission to transfer his funds. Our ignorance is increasingly behind the curve. The Global South has huge markets, entrepreneurial energy, and more innovations underway than we in the West often think. But its continued growth depends on many factors.

Sheer access is one. The International Telecommunication Union estimates that over 90 percent of people in developed countries have used the internet, but only 57 percent of people across developing countries. In LDCs this rate drops to 27 percent. A UN Pulse report on the Sustainable Development Goals notes that mobile networks still leave 8 percent of people in sub-Saharan Africa without coverage.

Western firms have nonetheless recognized the South's potential. According to DataReportal, nine of Facebook's ten biggest audiences are Global South countries. Netflix has started buying African and Middle Eastern content to maintain its market position. Plenty of innovation and growth is also homegrown. Southeast Asia has become a hub for mobile technology and ecommerce. Brazil and Chile are investing in wind and solar power. Gulf countries are pushing AI and blockchain. Africa has advanced in mobile communication and fintech. Kenya's mobile payment system M-Pesa shows how entrepreneurs in developing countries create tech solutions to everyday challenges. Writing in the *African Journal of Science, Technology, Innovation and Development*, Professor Timothy Waema noted that M-Pesa once channeled more transactions in Kenya in a day than Western Union did in the entire world.

Beyond digital, Saudi Arabia's smart city project "Neom" points to the level of ambition, creativity, and resources that some countries—at least in the upper income bracket—can mobilize. Its car-free city would run entirely on clean energy and be optimized by artificial intelligence. India has made strides in its space program. Its advances in biotechnology were apparent when it became one of the world's largest COVID vaccine suppliers.

Yet no opportunity comes without challenges. Yawning gaps persist between North and South—and within the South—in resources to support entrepreneurship, R&D, and, importantly, infrastructure on which innovation can build. The unequal distribution of technologies between urban and rural areas favors innovation in cities. Rural areas fall further behind, intensifying disparities.

For the Global South to sustain development, it will need both the public and private sectors to engage. Big multinationals from both East and West, however, prioritize their own interests. They seek to profit from fewer data regulations and push weaker domestic competitors aside. To some observers the provision of infrastructure, hardware, and software—be it from the US, Europe, or China—resembles the colonial railway projects Europeans pursued to render extraction from their overseas dependencies easier. "Digital colonialism" has become a watchword.

Even with all the right investments and reforms, technological success will ultimately depend on how well the Global South and its partners answer the fundamental challenge of equity. North-South cooperation must support the South's independence and help narrow, not widen, societal disparities. And the world must break its fixation on established Northern hubs to recognize transformative potential elsewhere.

Geopolitics—A Canvas of Interests
At the World Economic Forum in 2023, I met with around fifty diverse leaders to discuss the theme: "Preparing for a New Geopolitical Era Today." The rules were Chatham House—no comments attributed publicly without consent—the table set for an amicable yet frank debate.

The entire first half of the discussion focused on the war in Ukraine. I watched frustration deepening in the eyes of my colleagues from the Global South. Suddenly one of them stood up.

"I thought this was about a new geopolitical era, but all we are doing is talking about Ukraine," she said. "You all just don't get it, do you? The world has changed, but you have not."

The minister was right, of course. The Global West was so preoccupied with our own neighborhood that we failed to see beyond it.

Yet that moment of frustration also exposed an opportunity for the Global South. As the West and East have rearranged alliances and sought to rally support over Ukraine, the South has found a fresh platform to draw attention to its concerns. The South's collective bargaining power is at its peak. Its prospects for using that leverage to its ultimate benefit, however, are complicated.

Think of it like this: If consensus building in the EU's 27 nations is annoyingly painful, how should one expect a group of 125 states scattered across the globe to come close to a common agenda? Which interests do the 39 small island states share with the 32 landlocked developing countries? What goals could unite the commodity-export-dependent Arab and African economies and the diversified South Asian economies? Why would Peru, Namibia, or Sri Lanka have a stake in supporting Brazil, South Africa, or India's geopolitical ambitions? Why should the latter three keep the former three on board when negotiating new cooperation?

One answer came with Russia's war in Ukraine, which turbocharged a dynamic started in 2017, when the Trump administration signaled the return of "great power competition." Russia and China were already pushing that program. But now US allies and opponents alike had to show for whom they would root in this competition. Cold War–like bloc building was in the air. Russia's invasion heightened the pressure to choose sides. In a telling response, Uganda's UN ambassador Adonia Ayebare tried to stake out a third position. After abstaining from the first UN vote in early 2022, he tweeted: "As incoming Chair of the Non-aligned Movement (NAM) NEUTRALITY is key. Uganda will continue to play a constructive role in the maintenance of peace and security both regionally and globally."

Now, the shared purpose that brought cohesion to the Global South in the 1970s had a reason to exist again—to protect developing countries' interests against outsized actions of the East and West.

The Non-Aligned Movement itself is today a loosely organized forum with a rotating chairmanship, operating on consensus. Yet its neutrality is not always so simple. As East-West tensions mount, Global South countries must do an increasingly delicate dance to protect their interests without running afoul of big powers. For example, South Africa's supposed neutrality came into question when it conducted a naval exercise with Russia and China in 2023 and allowed a Russian cargo vessel under US sanctions to dock in a South African port. Then South Africa hosted a BRICS Summit—which it ultimately arranged for Putin not to attend. Putin did not attend the 2025 BRICS Summit in Brazil, either.

What has emerged since February 2022 is what we might call "tactical non-alignment," an approach that avoids the costs of engaging on any one side and profits from concessions offered by both. India's External Affairs Minister Subrahmanyam Jaishankar takes the idea further. He has criticized historic achievements of the Non-Aligned Movement and promoted "multi-alignment" instead. In his 2020 book *The India Way*, Jaishankar concluded: "[T]his is a time for us to engage America, manage China, cultivate Europe, reassure Russia, bring Japan into play, draw neighbors in, extend the neighborhood." Since the war began, India has successfully walked this tightrope.

If the war in Ukraine has provided the Global South with leverage, it has also shown its vulnerability. The COVID pandemic did likewise. Trade narrowed within a widening net of US and EU sanctions. Western governments' solutions, including domestic stimulus packages and friendshoring, stood to hurt emerging markets. The political energy and resources of the world's most powerful states were channeled into a regional conflict. Global challenges like climate change, poverty, and development had to wait.

The Global South's current approach reveals three central demands: First, to have more voice on the global stage. This means reform of the UN Security Council, which grants disproportionate influence to a tiny group of mid-twentieth-century powers. Beyond the UN, many Global South leaders also worry that small, exclusive clubs like the G7 can dictate the international agenda and want more inclusive fora. The G20 was a good start but not the final answer.

The second demand is a level economic and technological playing field. Given vastly different states of development, however, leveling requires support for the weak wherever possible and restraint for the strong where necessary. This includes fairer prices for raw materials, a more reciprocal opening of markets, and more generous sharing of technological advances. The WTO's creation in 1995 has contributed to a surge of global trade. Yet WTO reform is essential to make its rules more responsive to emerging markets.

A third demand is for a general overhaul of multilateralism. This means reform of the World Bank and IMF, where developing countries have close to no influence. A fairer multilateral system would also restrain the "weaponization" of international systems. American or European appeals to a rules-based order ring hollow if the West, through control of the dollar and international financial channels, can unilaterally decide to exclude others.

The Global South's campaign includes DIY diversification and greater regional integration. BRICS, for example, has pledged to strengthen their independence by pushing alternative currencies, developing their own global communication infrastructure, and cooperating on AI. The forum holds strong appeal for the Global South and has expanded from five to ten members, plus a partnership category that currently lists nine countries. China's vice minister of foreign affairs explained that BRICS "was inclusive . . . in sharp contrast to some countries' small circle." (Not naming names.)

A similar set of countries helped create the New Development Bank, a BRICS offshoot, and the Asian Infrastructure Investment Bank as alternatives to the IMF and World Bank to provide financial assistance without attaching political conditions. Their backers envision them becoming part of a new international financial architecture removed from Western control. A broader drive for regionalization reflects consensus that regional cooperation in trade, economics, and politics is essential to fuel growth and strengthen the Global South's resilience.

China is a driving force behind many of these initiatives, presenting itself as a leader of the non-Western world, East *and* South. Beijing is headquarters to the Shanghai Cooperation Organization on trade and regional security and the Asian Infrastructure Investment Bank. Shanghai hosts the New Development Bank and the BRICS Tower.

China likes to portray itself when convenient as a developing country and champion of the decolonization narrative. Yet its real ambition is to mold the international system, including the UN, in its own image. For big players in the Global South, especially India, China thus presents a challenge. Reform of the international order may be a shared goal—but China's own ambition as a hegemon is not.

Conclusion
When pressed to explain his country's position on the Ukraine war, India's External Affairs Minister Subrahmanyam Jaishankar declared: "I am not sitting on the fence just because I don't agree with you. It means I am sitting on my ground."

He stands for a new assertiveness with which Global South countries are demanding to be understood not as a function of East-West power politics but on their own terms.

Plenty of opportunities appear. For infrastructure funds the Global South can choose between the Chinese Belt and Road Initiative, the EU's Global Gateway, or the G7's Partnership for Global Infrastructure and Investment—to name but one area where great power competition may open options for developing countries.

The risks, on the other hand, are substantial. China never was a traditional non-aligned country. Today its outsized geopolitical weight worries its neighbors. More generally, the disproportionate strength of certain countries threatens to undercut the strength of the group. Sometimes referred to as the "graduation problem," countries with an economic advantage, like Brazil or India, might prioritize relations with economically powerful players over the pursuit of a common Global South agenda. Smaller and poorer states, in turn, remain susceptible to attempts to be bought off.

Nor is the Global South immune from the consequences of Russia's war on Ukraine. Were Putin to succeed, powerful actors everywhere might feel emboldened to deploy military might to redraw borders or establish regional hegemony. An obvious question would arise about China's ambitions in Taiwan, but the principle would apply anywhere.

Maybe the most central question that arises across the Global South is how to harness the biggest and most important resource it has: a young, growing, hopeful, and ambitious population. Demands for economic development, sustainable growth, fair trade, access to infrastructure and technology, and stability are already loud in developing countries and unwise to ignore.

It may not be for anybody in the East or West to tell the Global South how to achieve such conditions. Yet the more I listen to leaders from the Global South, the more I understand that the keys that will unlock the new world order are in their countries' hands.

Part Three
Dynamics

Competition

For Finland there is nothing more gratifying than beating Sweden in ice hockey, and never more so than in the world championship in Stockholm in 1995. It was Finland's first world championship—won against Sweden on Swedish home soil. It felt like a kind of proof that Finland, a small country still building on its liberation from Russia's shadow, had arrived. I watched that match in my dorm in Belgium, while schoolmates wondered why I was jumping up and down.

Finns and Swedes love each other before and after every match, but in between we want to beat each other—and not only in sports. Swedish Ericsson and Finnish Nokia spurred each other to become the world's two biggest mobile phone companies and later networks. Over the years our brotherly rivalry has helped us develop into two of the world's most modern countries.

In fact, all the Nordic countries—Denmark, Finland, Iceland, Norway, and Sweden—often find themselves in the top rankings on wealth, equality, environment, freedom, justice, and education. That, combined with some of the world's lowest income inequality, makes the Nordics lifestyle superpowers. Competition has been a key driver.

I always remind my Nordic friends that Finland has ranked as the happiest country in the world for eight years running (2018–2025). Yet competitive as I am, I must confess that all the Nordics can claim high happiness rankings. My Danish, Swedish, Norwegian, and Icelandic friends are, I'm sure, naturally just happy that we are so happy. And the competition goes on...

In decades past, we understood which players were likely to win the global economic and geopolitical games. The rules were clear, and there were certain competitors who, like the Florida Panthers or the Nordic cross-country skiers or the Jamaican sprinters, were well positioned to dominate.

That playing field has changed. The era of dominant global powers is giving way to a multipolar world of increasing competition. The competition plays out on many levels: between states, between regions, and between spheres of power. While the big picture is about the Global West, Global East, and Global South, a close-up look shows that the great US-China rivalry sits alongside regional competition for dominance among a host of other emerging powers.

The result is that today's competition is less stable than yesterday's, buffeted by the emergence of competing regional orders and alliances. If you are a small state, like Finland, your capacity to project power is limited. By joining a bigger regional entity, your influence grows. Organizations such as the African Union and ASEAN provide smaller states with insurance against being pushed around by the great powers. In increasingly transactional international politics, these fora multiply the options for smaller players to impact the international agenda.

All of this makes the outcome of the match less certain. In the coming decades, competition could lead in one of two ways: toward cooperation or conflict. The outcome will hinge on our ability to leverage competition as a force for positive development rather than mutual detriment. How? Competition can be a force for good only if we build a new rules-based global order that balances interests across the Global West, East, and South. If we succeed, competition could drive us all forward toward a more prosperous, equitable, and democratic world. If we fail, we spiral into trade war, hybrid war, and potentially conventional war.

These three dynamics of power—competition, conflict, and cooperation—will determine the order and balance of power between the Global West, East, and South. Unquestionably, all three will remain in play; they exist simultaneously and are deeply interconnected. Competition can spill into conflict unless it is contained by cooperation. Conflict makes both competition and cooperation difficult, sometimes impossible. Cooperation can foster fair play to support healthy competition and prevent it from becoming conflict.

The key to building a thriving world is to tilt the balance of competition toward cooperation rather than conflict. This last section of the book examines each of these forces and how they could play out. In this chapter, we begin with competition. I'll zoom in on four areas—political, economic, technological, and geopolitical—and explore the upsides and downsides of the competitive climate, both regionally and globally, for our shared future.

Competition enables innovation. Innovation enables growth. Growth enables welfare. At the same time, competition, both within and among states, requires the right balance. A balance between freedom and control, between monopoly and fragmentation, between expansion, domination, and fairness. This balance is never static. It is a moving target to which all players, from states to companies to civil society, must adjust.

Competing Political Systems

In 2008, as Finland's foreign minister, I met one-on-one with Islam Karimov, late president of Uzbekistan—though it was really more of a two-hour monologue than a meeting. I got in about five minutes on the importance of democracy. Karimov told me, in no uncertain terms, that the West did not need to come to Tashkent to lecture about values. I tried to say that values, including human rights, are universal. His eyes disagreed.

I left the meeting shaken. Karimov was a notorious dictator. He allegedly let his security service boil two prisoners to death and deliver the bodies to their families. He clung to power for twenty-five years. I still heartily hope that something, anything really, will bring down dictatorships like his. And indeed, when I met the current president of Uzbekistan, Shavkat Mirziyoyev, sixteen years later, things were changing.

Traveling home, I almost felt my heart warming at the thought that the worst that could happen to me as a politician in Finland is to get voted out of office. I thought to myself (and still do): democracy is right, dictatorship is wrong, plain and simple.

But I know that self-certain lectures won't be enough to protect democracy. The global competition among political systems depends on much more.

Yes, in a competitive world, even our political models are in contest. Democratic and autocratic states are engaged in a contest of narratives over which system is best. They compete over ideology, values, and the capacity to deliver prosperity, security, and welfare. Naturally, each model claims superiority. China boasts about its stability and economic strategy, while the United States trumpets its rapid innovation. Oil-and-gas-rich countries like Qatar and Saudi Arabia tout their growth and per-capita GDP. Nordic countries, including mine, brag about our high quality of life and low income inequality.

Claims of success sometimes rest on good arguments, sometimes on blunt propaganda. Legitimacy may come from fact-based comparisons, done by impartial international institutions or universities. But narratives (real or fabricated) count as much, sometimes more. To navigate the coming challenges effectively, we need to see beyond the popularity contest. We in the West mainly prefer democracy, but we must still understand and respect the context in which autocracy arises.

I believe firmly in democracy, rooted in regular elections, the separation of powers, a free press, and the protection of minorities through the rule of law. In this sense I am not impartial. Democracy might be inherently messy, but its historical track record is superior to that of most other systems. It outperforms autocracies in freedom of speech and civil liberties. It has lower levels of corruption and higher accountability. The V-Dem Institute's *Case for Democracy Report* cites evidence that after twenty-five years, a country that has transitioned toward democracy has on average 20 percent higher GDP per capita than an undemocratic country. Social spending increases in democratizing countries; so does access to education and gender equality. Infant mortality decreases significantly. I have personally participated in seven elections for European and Finnish office—and won only some. I did not complain either way.

The bottom line is that democracy is always a test—a challenge by nature, designed to forge compromise and navigate tensions between majorities and minorities. Yet it enshrines the essential values of individual freedom, political participation, and representation. Leaders are generally held accountable. Power transitions peacefully. Democracy has been good at creating prosperity, and certainly better than other systems at creating individual opportunity. But the balance is never perfect, often fragile.

The logic of autocracy is different. In an autocracy, power is concentrated in the hands of one or some individuals, not shared. There are no checks and balances. Autocracies can take many forms, including monarchies (Saudi Arabia), authoritarian one-party states (China), or military dictatorships (Myanmar). Autocratic rule typically entails a lack of free speech and political freedom, limited civil liberties, and no free, let alone fair, elections. Individual rights come second to what the autocratic regime calls the collective good.

It would be a simplification to say that autocracies do not deliver security, stability, or welfare. Many do. The more relevant question is how they do it and at what price to their people. Autocracies often claim there is a trade-off between freedom and security. They claim superiority at providing stability under adverse conditions, such as a pandemic or a population divided by ethnic or religious factions. And they are not necessarily wrong.

Don't get me wrong, I am not prepared to ditch my Western values on the altar of geopolitical interests. I do say, though, that it's a mistake to condemn undemocratic countries without deepening our understanding of the historical and cultural roots of diverging systems of governance. Too often we believe that our own experience can be generalized and projected onto others. We forget that it took centuries for many European nations to create the institutions and habits of democracy. We overlook how much easier it is to focus on individual freedoms when we have the basic needs of food, infrastructure, and medicine.

Simple as the distinction between political systems may appear, the global picture is hardly binary. The world's nations represent a broad array of competing political ideologies and practices. Many systems are democracy-autocracy hybrids. Some so-called democracies in the Global West flirt with an illiberal form of democracy that tips into autocracy. Some Global South countries are much more democratic than others in the West. And the Global East is about more than autocracy.

This is where competition comes into play—a tournament of global public opinion. Almost everything in the modern world can be measured, often in real time. The list of state rankings includes PISA, the World Press Freedom Index, the Environmental Performance Index, the Human Development Index, and countless more ways to check scores on which states or regions are doing better than others.

Ultimately, the winning odds of any political system hinge on delivery. There are trade-offs and priorities in every system. Stability and security may come at the cost of freedom and innovation. Growth may come at the cost of social equality. Participation and representation may come at the cost of speed and efficiency. Competition often turns into a contest of narratives, where leaders justify limitations in one area with progress in others.

Prosperity, however, remains among the core measures for any system. This is why competing political models are so closely linked to economic competition.

Competing Economic Models

After the Cold War the Global West felt that it had won not only the political battle, but also the economic one. I remember sitting in EU meetings as a young civil servant in the late 1990s, listening to sermons about the virtues of the free movement of goods, services, labor, and capital. I continued those sermons myself as a Member of the European Parliament in the mid-2000s. Part of the thinking on globalization went that the economic pie was getting bigger and bigger. Competition might dictate that slices of the pie would grow at different rates for each country, but they would all grow after all. Companies would invest in regions with stable governments and predictable regulations. Competition could have a democratizing effect.

While not all those assumptions were wrong, today, zero-sum thinking has returned. In the lingering ripples of global recession, growth has stayed slow. Just as important, the gains from technological advances and free trade have been unevenly shared. Populist politicians of the far right and left look for scapegoats—economic competitors and often immigrants. Many people believe that their neighbors' gains come at the cost of their own losses.

States need to grow to provide domestic welfare. The better the economy, the easier it is to deliver basic social security, and thus the more likely that a given regime stays in power. But if the pie is not growing, the need to develop a competitive edge over other states becomes more urgent. Competition becomes fiercer. Economic nationalism has returned.

Economic competition amid today's disorder is also less stable than it was in the post–Cold War era. The rules for global trade are weaker and less respected. Free markets have been partially replaced with forms of state capitalism. These trends only accelerated during the crisis decade encompassing the global financial crisis, the pandemic, and Russia's attack on Ukraine. Now societies are less willing to compromise in the short run in the hope of long-term gains.

Each of the world's largest economies positions itself differently within this context—effectively placing its own bet for success.

The EU's early economic success was based on the Common Market: free internal movement, competition, and trade. In the 2000s, the focus shifted to building a knowledge-based economy driven by innovation and research. This focus has not changed radically, but the world has. Protectionist and interventionist tendencies in the EU are now on the rise. Maybe the EU's biggest asset is its regulatory capacity, the so-called "Brussels Effect." Any multinational company that wants access to the EU's twenty-seven member states, the world's biggest market, must abide by EU rules. Provided that regulations overall improve rather than stifle competition—a constant balancing act between overregulation and underregulation—this gives the EU a competitive edge globally. Yet competing regulatory spaces are already on the horizon.

The US economy has always been characterized by free markets, private ownership, and competition, with government involvement seen as inimical to innovation. The Biden-era Inflation Reduction Act and CHIPS Act, which poured billions of dollars into infrastructure, clean energy, and technology, were classic state interventionism. The second Trump administration is leaning even more protectionist, threatening tariffs on friends and foes alike. At the time of this writing, the risk of a trade war runs high, but the end result can also be positive: removal of trade barriers by mutual agreement. The EU must work to this end.

Free markets and competition have served the US well: the model has produced some of history's most admired and successful multinationals, like Apple, Microsoft, Amazon, and Google, to name but the biggest. The system favors entrepreneurship and rewards private investment. There is no startup scene more impressive than in Silicon Valley. However, like any economic model, the American one has its downsides.

Since my formative years at Furman University, I have always admired the United States. But as agile as the system might be, I worried about its distributive power—or more precisely, the lack thereof. A firm believer in Nordic welfare capitalism, I have seen up close that the American system is good at creating wealth but poor at distributing it fairly. Social security networks are practically nonexistent, as is public health care. Visiting the US in the 2020s feels like going back to the 1990s. The US is not a modern society by European or Asian standards. The infrastructure is antiquated. Cars are absurdly big. Homelessness and poverty are widespread. Without radical change toward a basic welfare state, the political polarization will continue.

In the Global East, China's economic system is a hybrid, often referred to as "Socialism with Chinese Characteristics," but more aptly described as state capitalism. The government is instrumental in planning and directing the economy and maintains control over strategic sectors, including telecommunications and banking. At the same time, it allows market forces to drive innovation. China has been good at copying best practices from different economic models around the world. By continuously modernizing its economy, China has become an exporter of sophisticated smartphones alongside large-scale infrastructure projects and the finance to go with them—all while constraining the activities of foreign companies in its domestic market.

There is, however, a question of sustainability. Demography is no longer on China's side. With an aging population, fewer young people work and more old people require care. President Xi believes in a model of dual circulation. He banks on the size of China's domestic consumption (internal circulation) and drives international trade and investment (external circulation). Time will tell whether this strategy works in the long run.

Admittedly, I have never had much faith in the Russian economy. I saw it for the first time when I visited Moscow in 1983. I was a teenager, playing for the Helsinki ice hockey team. In the Soviet Union, the cars looked old, cigarettes smelled bad, and hotels had guards on each floor. Only two consumer goods were of interest for a Westerner: vodka and caviar. You could buy these with foreign currency or an old pair of jeans. After our hockey games, which we lost, the Russian players would rush to us to exchange hockey sticks. We agreed out of courtesy and were left with sticks best used as kindling on cold winter nights.

My perception of the Russian economy has not changed much. The post-1990 reforms were abrupt, the transition from a centrally planned to a market economy chaotic. As state-owned companies privatized, corrupt oligarchs took over key industries with government support. The gap between rich and poor grew to unprecedented levels. I hoped change would finally arrive around 2000. But Putin's ascent to become an unchecked autocrat with imperial ambitions set different priorities. He went for symbolic projects, like the unsuccessful Skolkovo, instead of structural modernization. Russia today remains a petrostate. Rather than rallying domestic consumption and entrepreneurship, it will become ever more dependent on energy exports to the Global East and South.

The story of the Global South is mixed. Geography, demographics, and development differ across countries and continents. Their economic approaches range from market-oriented economies like Mexico, Brazil, or South Africa, to state-controlled economies like Vietnam or Angola. The West may preach free trade and privatization as a one-size-fits-all solution, but the needs of Global South economies have differed greatly across time and space. Some, like Brazil, India, or South Africa, clearly became winners of globalization. Others are still struggling to keep their heads above water.

The Global South's competitive edge today lies in its abundant supplies of raw materials and its growth potential. These assets are unevenly distributed, and the African continent, given its young, fast-growing population and possession of key minerals, might just have the best prospects. But instability, conflict, and corruption remain major obstacles on its path. India seems to be avoiding these pitfalls and is on track to become a robustly growing large economy. What is clear, though, is that the Global South is fully buying neither the Western model of a liberal economy nor the heavy-handed state approach of the East. It seeks a middle way and continues to watch which system shows greater resilience to current strains.

It is relatively straightforward to measure competitiveness in economic indicators such as GDP, growth, productivity, trade, and inflation. But today's competition will be about more than scores in these categories. Control over the rules and instruments of the global economy is itself a contest. Those who determine trade rules, write WTO and IMF policy, or sit on the UN Security Council influence the entire playing field. In a zero-sum game, everyone fights to win. Whoever sets the rules gains the advantage.

The Contest for Technological Hegemony

When I started framing this book in 2020, I focused on technology's impact on governance. Would we end up with digital democracies or digital dictatorships? Then many things changed. We lived through the COVID-19 pandemic. We saw Russia invade Ukraine. War erupted between Israel and Hamas. Donald Trump was reelected president.

At the same time, great power competition unfolded in the sphere of technology. Throughout history, technology has driven both political power and economic growth. States with a technological edge, be that the printing press or steam engine or computer, are always ahead of the economic curve—which gives them political power. Now we can add to that list: artificial intelligence, quantum computers, satellites, data centers, and more.

Democracies and authoritarian regimes today face a common challenge: Technology changes everything. Innovations are already transforming our economies, militaries, science, politics, and the way we live. The resulting disruptions and accelerations have the power to make or break economies and even regimes, depending on how technology is encouraged or constrained.

The key question is how different states, companies, and international organizations will cope with this force of disruption—leveraging technology's advantages while containing its threats. Is the recipe pouring state funds into projects and orchestrating innovation (China)? Or allowing the markets to take the lead (the US)? Or finding the right regulations to let technology grow yet manage its disruption (the EU)?

Speaking broadly, autocratic states are vulnerable because they can't control technology as much as they want to, and democracies are vulnerable because they don't want to control technology as much as they need to. The right course might just lie somewhere in the middle.

Let's look at one particularly instructive example of technological competition: data. Data can unlock powerful economic growth and political advantage. But it also represents a serious vulnerability, as it exposes governments and businesses to cyberattacks, spying, and sabotage.

There are three basic approaches. China centralizes data within government, which mines data without restriction for the benefit of the state. In the US, private companies can mine data, at least theoretically based on some form of individual consent. Europe puts data sovereignty first. Data ownership lies with the individual, and its use is closely regulated and monitored. The European approach is probably ethically strongest and competitively weakest.

Data feeds competition on several levels. Economically, "big data" is an enormous resource. US firms like Google or Meta pioneered data mining and finding ways to profit from it. In China, companies like Tencent, Alibaba, and ByteDance (TikTok) quickly caught up and became global competitors. But the Chinese government recognized the potential of data mining, too. Its social governance strategy relies on collecting and analyzing data on individuals and businesses through a Social Credit System that issues "trustworthiness" scores. Government can thus reach deep into citizens' private lives and exert wide-ranging powers over firms.

There is no European company able to compete on the same level. The European Union has recognized this disadvantage and launched the "European Digital Decade," trying to protect citizens' data sovereignty while enabling digital industry to flourish—though this has yet to improve the EU's economic position.

Data dynamics have already revealed the overlap between technological and geopolitical competition. Western powers concerned over data security and infrastructure have banned (US) or strictly regulated (EU) certain digital services from China. 5G is a classic example, where close ties between the private company Huawei and the Chinese government sparked fears that China would use its access to spy or subvert digital networks abroad.

Yet competition is still on as far as emerging markets are concerned. Whereas China can provide fast and cheaper network infrastructure and user devices, Western brands like Apple still carry more prestige. The geopolitical rivals are keenly aware of the hard and soft power potentials that lie in technology cooperation.

The US ban on exporting chips to China is something like a summary of the conflict and competition raging in technology. It aims to curtail growth in China's military capabilities by slowing semiconductor and AI development—but also to weaken China's ability to serve foreign partners and slow the expansion of Chinese brands. The measure's bluntness speaks to the stakes at play.

Beyond data, geopolitical rivalry fuels fierce competition in machine learning, blockchain, cloud computing, cybersecurity, bioinformatics, genomics, space technology, and advanced manufacturing. For some, AI raises echoes of Orwell's *1984*. They see a straight line between digitalization and the rise of an autocratic, all-controlling system. I strongly disagree. Technology is what we make of it. This is why I believe the EU's approach is right, even if it might slow market forces for innovation, and even if it needs adaptation to the competitive landscape.

The most successful states, in the end, will be those that find the right equilibrium.

Geopolitical Competition

Geopolitics—the study of how geography (including location, resources, and size) interplays with political power—used to be a rather straightforward affair. Most countries seemed to be on a gradual track toward peaceful interdependence. The geopolitical contest faded into the background.

Now geopolitics is back, in a way I have not seen for thirty years. The reasons are Russia's attack on Ukraine and the rivalry between the US and China.

The integration we heralded after the Cold War also created countless new mechanisms of competition. We used to equate power with hard power, especially military capacity. Today soft and smart power pack almost as much punch. Military matters, but so does innovation. Natural resources matter, but so does trading power. Alliances matter, but so does the capacity to set global security rules and project the image of success.

Companies today increasingly complement market studies with geopolitical analysis—because conflict disrupts markets, supply chains, and consumption. Private and public-sector actors want a forecast, not just on profit but global dynamics. I see many companies hiring "chief geopolitical officers." The definition of geopolitics has changed.

The major players in the Global West, East, and South bring their own strategies to this contest, each pursuing the prize of dominance, each with its own strengths and weaknesses.

The US still has pretty much all the instruments it needs. Its geography provides protection, its terrain is rich in raw materials, its economy produces innovation and wealth. On defense, it outspends China, Russia, and the next seven countries—combined. Its Achilles' heel is an unstable and polarized political system, which has left allies and adversaries alike worried about sudden policy shifts.

The EU used to shy away from hard power and focus on soft and smart power. But the European Commission under Ursula von der Leyen has shifted. It pictures itself as a geopolitical player and has many instruments at its disposal. The EU is a global heavyweight in trade and regulation. Its monetary and financial influence allowed it, with the US, to exclude Russia from major finance markets after February 2022. Its most powerful geopolitical tool, however, may still be its enlargement policy. The EU's image nourishes among neighboring countries the desire to join. And these countries accept a host of rules and conditions to become a member.

Now the Commission is also stepping up European defense, partially forced by President Trump's "America First" drive. The EU peace project has suddenly become a "war" project. Donald Trump did more in five weeks to force Europe to take responsibility for its own security than US presidents in the past fifty years.

China has scale and size, economic and military power. Its global Belt and Road Initiative has involved some 150 countries, at times executing infrastructure projects with awe-inspiring speed and efficiency. China's political system seems on its face more stable than that of the US, and certainly more predictable. Part of modern geopolitics is the ability to use instruments of power consistently. China does. The US—due to the pendulum swings of a two-party democracy—does not. China's newer, and still somewhat aspirational, role as mediator in geographically distant conflicts underscores its growing geopolitical weight.

Russia remains a top-tier geopolitical player. But for how much longer? It has oil, gas, and minerals and is the go-to security exporter for many countries. Its military has modernized through the war in Ukraine. Yet many countries already treat it as a political pariah. Its war economy has shown resilience toward Western sanctions, but the forces of economic renewal seem all but dead. Energy offers a good metaphor for Russia's geopolitical role: it is consuming resources it cannot sustain.

Invisible, interconnected levers of power have become more important than ever. Control of maritime routes and strategic chokepoints remains crucial. Yet previously quiet elements of international relations—setting rules for international traffic, trade, and finance, dictating climate targets, managing security cooperation across regions, and influencing the institutions that oversee international monitoring and arbitration—are now factors in the geopolitical competition. States with power in institutions like the IMF or WTO, namely the US and Western Europe, can protect their interests. But this position of influence comes at a cost of global trust.

In this context, we have also seen alliances shift—or a competition for alliances, if you will. After its Ukraine attack, Russia was isolated from the Global West. It shifted cooperation toward the Global East and South. Yet other countries are cautious in cooperating with Russia to avoid facing sanctions themselves. The war brought the transatlantic alliance closer together but still left it unable to build the global alliance it hoped for.

In this atmosphere of contention and latent conflict, some middle or emerging powers, such as Iran, South Africa, Qatar, and the United Arab Emirates, are now punching above their traditional geopolitical weight. Economically heavier players, like Brazil, India, and Saudi Arabia, are catching up with first-rank geopolitical players like the EU. Even if the US and China continue to be in a league of their own, geopolitical power has become relative.

Conclusion

In the new world order, competition can either be a force for good (healthy development) or ill (destructive conflict). It can be a race to the top or a race to the bottom.

Competing political systems are good if comparisons and contrasts fuel ambition and lead to improvements. At the moment, however, democracies are instead facing domestic challenges from rising populism.

Economic competition is good when it incentivizes innovation, development, and growth. The problem is that many less-developed states see competition as unfair. Economic competition is swinging away from Western models, as states across the political spectrum turn inward, restricting trade and digging deeper into state control.

Technologically, competition drives innovation and growth. The question is: to what end? Whether it fuels good or bad outcomes is up to us. We may find ways to contain technological competition for mutual benefit. Otherwise, unevenly regulated technology will feed a descent into digital dictatorships or new forms of warfare.

The trends are worrisome. The trajectory points to an uneven playing field, deepening insularity and mistrust, and a waning ability to forge shared solutions to problems that confront us all.

Marshalling competition as a force for good requires revitalizing the rules-based global order with a fairer distribution of power that balances varying global interests. For novel fields, we need new rules and models of governance. We will succeed only if we forge them together. If states do not trust each other to fairly set or follow the rules, then competition becomes difficult to contain. This is the point where competition risks escalating into conflict.

Conflict

Christmas Day, 2024. I'm at the dinner table with my family when I get a message from the situation room: four cables connecting Estonia and Finland have been cut in the Baltic Sea. This is the fifth incident in less than two years.

Within hours, Finnish authorities identify two ships that could have caused the damage. One is approaching the Balticconnector gas pipeline—which could mean even more carnage. Time is of the essence.

Finnish vessels identify the ship as crude oil tanker Eagle S, *registered in the Cook Islands. It departed Russia the previous day. Seeing the ship's anchor down, our officials request it to move from international into Finnish waters. The crew complies. And in our waters we exercise our right to board and impound it for criminal investigation.*

Investigators will later find a sixty-mile anchor drag mark on the sea floor. There are three possible explanations: accident, intent, or incompetence. Or perhaps a combination of all three.

> *Hybrid warfare—cyberattacks, sabotage, and disinformation—is now part of the playbook of state and non-state actors alike. The aim is to cause mayhem. To throw the target off-balance.*
>
> *In this case, Finnish authorities stayed calm and prevented further carnage. Will we ever find out who was behind the incident? I leave that to the reader to judge.*
>
> *What we must all understand is that as interstate conflict grows and takes on new forms, we must act wisely—and act together across borders—to prevent it from spiraling into war.*

If I could time-travel back to Furman University in 1991 and describe today's world to my younger self, I would scarcely believe it.

I would have to explain that a Russian invasion of Ukraine broke the peace of Europe. That Hamas made a murderous incursion into southern Israel, killing around 1,200 soldiers and civilians and taking more than 250 hostages—and that Israel responded with a devastating military campaign that by early 2025 had killed tens of thousands of Palestinians, mostly women and children, and spilled into conflict in Lebanon and Iran. I would recount that divisions within Africa's Sahel region have merged with great power rivalries as Russia sought to disrupt Western efforts to contain the spread of jihadis. That Sudan is now (again) locked in a bloody civil war. And that, on the other side of the globe, Xi Jinping seems to have dropped China's hide-your-strength-and-bide-your-time strategy in favor of ever more demonstrations of military power to press reunification with Taiwan.

Those would only be the stories about *military* conflicts today. There are also economic conflicts (tariffs and sanctions), financial and infrastructure strikes (cyberattacks and sabotage), information wars (digital disinformation and propaganda across borders), and competitive diplomacy. Over the last thirty-five years, everything about conflict has changed, from the scale to the types of fighters to the way they fight.

This is not a world at peace. It is a world of rising tensions—which is to be expected when multilateral institutions are weakened and foreign relations increasingly transactional. Without clear rules, norms, and reliance on international institutions, competition becomes increasingly difficult to contain.

The multilateral institutions set up to prevent such conflicts, above all the UN, are not equipped to respond effectively to this new face of conflict. And they have, in the present wars in Ukraine, Israel-Palestine, and Sudan, proven largely powerless. Without clear leadership from an international institution, it's hard to achieve a peace deal that considers broader implications. Instead, big powers and smaller actors make deals that serve their own interests. Solutions become transactional and thus narrow and temporary.

The great responsibility for global leaders is to prevent tensions from erupting into outright conflict—and to prevent regional wars from going global. Success will depend on how well the world can cooperate, meaning: renew a rules-based international system that everyone can believe in and manage competition before it becomes conflict. We need to do that now—and do it nimbly enough to adapt to a world changing even as I write.

The Changing Nature of Conflict

The nature of conflict changed gradually enough that many of us, myself included, did not initially notice. During the Cold War, most wars were civil wars or proxy fights. The cost was horrific for those in war zones. But rich Western nations and the Soviet Union were directly affected only where they committed their own forces abroad. From then on, we believed, the only wars would be local.

So high was Western confidence in a peaceful future after the Cold War that NATO all but scrapped its traditional warfighting capacity in favor of smaller, cheaper expeditionary forces to underpin security in still-troubled regions. *Out of area or out of business*, the NATO slogan ran. Meanwhile, the UN retooled its security structures to address civil wars, not interstate wars.

Soon enough, however, local conflicts started to become regional. The US War on Terror succeeded in driving the Taliban from Afghanistan only to see the Islamist fundamentalists continue the war from Pakistan. The Arab Spring of 2011–2012, hailed by some as proof of the march of democracy, turned out to be the harbinger of several bloody civil wars. And France had to quit the fight against jihadis in Africa's Sahel region as democracies fell to Russian-backed coups.

At the same time, the focus of fighting shifted from interstate wars to non-state actors. Rebels and terrorist groups became the main target of state military action. The terrorist attacks of 9/11 triggered NATO's mutual-defense guarantee for the first time in history, activating a coalition to fight back. Crisis hotspots like Syria turned into complicated conflicts with regional and international dimensions. The US, meanwhile, learned that it is one thing to conquer a country, quite another to keep it conquered, and its body politic began to balk at the role of global police officer. China and Russia stepped into the emerging gap. For those paying attention, Russia's incursions into Georgia in 2008 and Crimea in 2014 were sure signs that the nature of conflict was changing. Finally, Russia's Ukraine invasion and the war in Israel-Palestine made the expansion from local to regional conflict too obvious to overlook. Interstate wars have returned.

Neither are the methods of warfare the same as they used to be. Israel has effectively won its war on technological superiority—at one point simultaneously exploding thousands of Hezbollah pagers across Lebanon at the push of a button in Tel Aviv. Russia and Ukraine are technologically well-versed in modern warfare. When Russia invaded, Ukrainians asked their allies for ammunition, air defenses, and missiles. By the war's third year, they were asking us to finance drone production. This is a glimpse of the future, and it has already arrived.

The international peace and security systems set up to prevent such conflicts, however, have been unable to adjust. Even UN peacekeeping structures redesigned during the War on Terror do not match the complex mix of players and settings we see today. Most conspicuously, the UN has found itself paralyzed on critical Security Council votes, as China and Russia veto resolutions on Ukraine and the US tends to veto those on Israel and Palestine. The vacuum leaves the field open to big-power politics, paving the way for Saudi Arabia to seek a transactional deal with Israel, or perhaps Russia to do so with the US. Iran also has played its role in Israel-Palestine, acting through proxy forces (the Houthis in Yemen, Hamas in Gaza, and Hezbollah in Lebanon) in pursuit of state interests.

New challenges require new tools. As interstate conflict resurges, it might be tempting to move backward, to resurrect peacekeeping models built after World War II. But it's clear that our present and future world demand we move forward. We need to remodel international conflict management systems to address the full range of conflict that we confront: state and non-state, internal and external, primary and proxy. And we must retrain ourselves to address weapons and strategies that I, as an aspiring young diplomat, could not have imagined—because along with the warring parties the methods of war itself have dramatically changed.

Hybrid Warfare
"I need ammunition, not a ride." This simple statement, given in reply to an American evacuation offer by Ukrainian President Volodymyr Zelenskyy as Russian forces crossed his border, is not only a symbol of Ukraine's resilience but a prime example of what is needed to succeed in modern warfare. Materiel, yes. But more important, a personalized message, homemade, delivering a morale boost to fighters and allies and a warning to enemies in the same sentence. Non-state groups and insurgencies had previously used such informal, grassroots tactics. But in those six words, Zelenskyy showed that these—along with a host of other nontraditional methods—were the province of warring governments, as well.

The return of war, in Gaza as well as Ukraine, has illuminated dramatic changes in the way it is fought. Where once we lost sleep over a single devastating weapon, now we must nimbly keep pace with the sheer number of available tools of conflict. Ironically, this proliferation springs in part from the global interconnectedness that we cultivated. The same interdependence that fosters growth and reduces poverty also vastly multiplies the tools with which one state can inflict damage and pain on another. Virtually everything, from information to technology, energy to currency, raw materials to migration, can be weaponized. Developments designed to bring nations together—open trade and investment markets, freer movement of labor, the accurately named "worldwide web"—can be bent to the cause of confrontation.

Hybrid warfare—including economic, technological, and psychological weapons—will shape our future conflicts and the way we fight them. There is no longer a clear line between conventional kinetic warfare and these more dispersed strategies, or between formal war and subtler acts of provocation. The boundaries are blurred. And all of us—leaders and citizens alike—need to be prepared.

Available tactics in hybrid warfare accumulated in recent decades as global relations descended into increasingly antagonistic forms of competition. Methods previously used by non-state actors are now commonly used by states against other states. Let's look at a partial list.

Economically, states or groups of states may apply sanctions, freeze individual or group assets, restrict access to financial markets, disrupt supply chains, or impose trade tariffs. Technologically, states hiding in the internet's shadowy corners can hack into foreign governments' or private companies' computer systems, steal information, and wreak havoc. Cyberattacks and acts of infrastructure sabotage like the one that disrupted my Christmas supper have become an ongoing front between countries that are not actually at war. In the arena of information, competition has become a battle of narratives, a contest for hearts and minds, dominated not only by national parties and politicians but increasingly infiltrated and abused by foreign powers. Social media, and more recently innovations in AI, amplify the power of disinformation. Even human migration can be wielded as a form of confrontation, where one country

(Russia) pressures its neighbor (Finland) by sending migrants—many of them conscripted to the task—across its borders.

Russia may lag in many technologies, but it has proven highly sophisticated at deploying such hybrid tactics. Its war on Ukraine illustrates the case. In one sense, it fits the traditional template of a territorial land grab. But in its prosecution Moscow has reached well beyond traditional war tools and beyond Ukraine's borders as it seeks to weaken international support for Ukraine. It attempts to destabilize US and European domestic politics by interfering in elections, seeding digital propaganda and misinformation, and funding political extremists. Tactics run from there along a spectrum to deliberate gas and energy disruptions, critical infrastructure attacks, and widespread cyber operations calculated to create economic disruption. In late 2024, Nordea, a bank used by roughly 30 percent of the Finnish population, endured seventy consecutive days of cyberattacks that succeeded in bringing down its system for twelve cumulative hours. US federal government and healthcare computer systems have also been hit. Who exactly perpetrated those attacks? Part of these tactics' effectiveness is that no one can say with certainty.

More overtly, Russia and Belarus have sought to weaponize irregular migration, offering a jumping-off point for western Europe to those fleeing conflicts in the Middle East and thus stoking the fires of populism and isolationism among Ukraine's allies. Finland closed its border with Russia because if we open it, Russia will likely fly thousands of asylum seekers from Yemen, Ethiopia, Eritrea, Syria, and Iraq in on chartered flights to overwhelm Finnish capacity and cause domestic tension.

The net effect is like the 2022 film *Everything Everywhere All at Once*. Traditional, kinetic warfare continues, as the people of Ukraine know only too well. But it is accompanied and complicated by a swirl of incursions in other arenas, many of them from sources hard to identify. The perpetrators' aim is to blur the boundary between peace and war—to deploy intimidation and coercion without formal declaration of hostilities. This poses a dilemma for adversaries. Does cutting a vital digital cable constitute an act of war that could lead NATO to activate mutual defense? How can we be certain that it represents a deliberate act of sabotage? Hybrid tactics muddy the waters and can lead to unexpected escalations.

For their part, the US and its Western allies have raised economic sanctions and financial offensives to new strength. Western powers have frozen Russia's financial assets—and are using the interest on them to finance weapons for Ukraine. Import and export prohibitions have shut down much of Russia's trade with the West, a hard hit for a national economy fueled by gas exports. Ukraine's allies have seized the Mayfair mansions and Mediterranean yachts of Russia's richest men.

The West is also flexing these muscles beyond Russia and applying them to show force to its quieter rival, China. Within the first six weeks of his second term, President Trump imposed trade tariffs on China. A series of US administrations, recognizing that military strength will rest on technological prowess, have restricted the sale of advanced silicon chips to China. Chinese companies are effectively locked out of the American tech sector. European nations, as well, have blocked Chinese takeovers of companies at the forefront of artificial intelligence.

The weaponization of everything delivers two important consequences beyond its intended targets. First, it further weakens the global order. Sanctions, for example, are not a new instrument but have rarely been applied with the intensity of those imposed on Russia by the EU and G7. They serve to pressure a warring party without engaging directly in war. Yet sanctions also carry risks for those imposing them. The dollar's role as the world's only reserve currency gives Washington unparalleled control of the international financial system, allowing it to force third countries to shut down payments to and from America's adversaries. But the more often the weapon is used, the greater the incentive for others to build alternative systems to bypass the dollar. China and Russia have already moved in that direction.

Second, Russia's war in Ukraine has demonstrated that the step from misinformation campaigns and cyberattacks to physical destruction is a small one and quickly done. In addition to Baltic Sea communications cables, acts of sabotage on EU countries have included arson and targeted energy grids and other critical infrastructure. It seems a miracle that none of these incidents has caused fatalities—yet. Future forms of sabotage could include biological agents that target public health. The weaponization of everything, in short, has reduced the distance between competition and conflict as the crumbling of global order has greatly increased the threat that smaller wars will ensnare great powers.

On the battlefield itself, technology promises to transform war—and is already doing so. Israel's victories over Hamas and Hezbollah hinged on technological superiority as much as conventional weaponry. The Israeli Defense Forces have tracked Hamas leaders using facial recognition technology, used aboveground geotechnology to map underground tunnels, and remotely exploded walkie-talkies in Hezbollah commanders' hands.

The Ukraine war has shown that armies still need rocket artillery and tanks to seize territory, but drones, cheap and quickly produced, have proven the most lethal weapon on both sides. When the war began, Ukraine produced few drones. In 2025 Ukraine aims to produce 4.5 million.

Beyond the horizon, drones, robots, and digitally directed fire systems will make fighting increasingly automated. Soldiers whose packs were once loaded with guns and ammunition will now be deployed operating lethal drones. Fighter pilots will sit behind consoles in remote locations to "fly" a new generation of warplanes. Warring parties will pursue these tactics in tandem with hybrid attacks that aim to destabilize citizens' lives at home.

Hybrid warfare directly strains civilians far from the battlefield in a way that kinetic, conventional warfare does not. The technological conveniences that we take for granted in our daily lives also make us vulnerable. Cyberattacks could block access to your money or medical prescriptions. Sabotage could cause an electrical blackout. A disinformation campaign could fill your social feeds with deepfakes that make you unsure of the truth. The chaos that results is exactly the point: to cause havoc that undermines public morale and political support.

All of which means that national security now relies more than ever on civilians' cognitive resilience. To counter such offensives, everyday people need the strength, wisdom, and steadiness to weather disruptions while keeping matters in perspective—to "keep calm and carry on," as my British in-laws might say. Societal resilience is now a matter of national security. We are all part of the defense.

Blurring Foreign and Domestic Policy

In Finland the constitution provides a nice division of labor between the president and the government. Put simply, the president does foreign policy together with the government and the government does domestic and EU policy without the president. Sounds tidy—except that the world is more complex. Is EU foreign policy Finnish foreign policy? Yes. Is an attack on a data cable in the Baltic Sea part of foreign policy? Certainly—but also internal security. In today's world, in Finland and everywhere, the line between foreign and domestic policy is always blurred.

Domestic dynamics today are both drivers and symptoms of the changing world order. Sometimes foreign policy can be best understood as shadowboxing in domestic politics.

The influence of domestic politics on foreign policy is not new. After all, the national mood of isolationism obliged President Franklin Roosevelt to delay US entry into World War II until Japan bombed Pearl Harbor. Democracy is about nothing if not public consent. But these days politicians ever more openly advertise their foreign policy stances as currency in domestic political debate. In this game, policy is no longer based on values but *value*—often narrowly interpreted. Witness both Trump's "America First" slogan and Biden's "Foreign Policy for the Middle Class." And the permeable boundaries between the domestic and foreign make it harder for us to prevent competition from sliding into conflict.

Why, for example, did Biden withdraw troops from Afghanistan at the scale and speed he did, despite the contrary advice of experienced foreign policy experts? Because most US citizens wanted it. Domestic pressure also played a role in the decision to enter Afghanistan in the first place in 2001. In the public mind, a terrorist attack as big as 9/11 cannot go unanswered—no matter the military or foreign policy implications of the response. The latest Israel-Hamas conflict starting in 2023, in turn, influenced national political agendas all over the world.

Sometimes surprising foreign policy shifts have roots in domestic dynamics. Take, for example, the early foreign policy of Trump's second term. Pressuring Ukraine was about ending the war quickly to free the US from its obligations and thus make good on a campaign promise. Calling for Europe to take on more of its own security was about reducing costs for American taxpayers. Getting a minerals deal with Ukraine was about proving that the president can forge agreements that benefit the US economy. All foreign policies driven by a domestic agenda—even if in an admittedly nontraditional style.

This blurring of foreign and domestic is not only a Western phenomenon. Several trends have pushed domestic concerns into foreign policy around the globe. A radical change in the media landscape is certainly one. Social media, blogs, influencers, and the 24/7 news cycle all play an outsize role. Never in human history has almost everyone on the planet had so much access to so much communication from virtually unlimited sources—or has that information been so easy to manipulate and spread.

As a head of state, I encounter this challenge every day. On the upside, modern media allows me to communicate directly with constituents about real-time events and tap into public conversation. The downside, however, is substantial. Anything I express is instantly tackled, pundit-ized, manipulated, and amplified within filter bubbles that drive public opinion to polar extremes. Civilians online face the same hurdles. Molehills become mountains. Mountains become domestic battlegrounds.

It's hard for societies to foster dialogue, forge common ground, or find lasting solutions—including in foreign relations.

Rising income inequality, as well, provides plenty of fuel for the informational fire. As median incomes in the US and most of Europe stagnated, the top 1 percent's riches multiplied. On the unfairness of this outcome, populists have a point. The danger of populism lies in its supposed remedies: aggressive nationalism, scapegoating immigrants and minorities, and weakening civil protections that underpin democracy. Simple solutions to complex problems. With hardly any checks on truth or fiction, populists selling simple messages pack an obvious advantage. If you say something often enough, people will begin to believe it.

Diasporas also press foreign and domestic policy together by creating microcosms of conflicts far from the battlefield. Arab Americans in the US state of Michigan, outraged at the Biden administration's support for Israel, helped deliver Donald Trump a victory over Vice President Kamala Harris. Internal religious politics in Pakistan are transposed onto UK society and politics. Turkish political tensions play out inside Germany, as do dynamics in the Sahel on domestic politics in France. This is not new on our small planet, but the more we connect across borders the more diaspora communities hold sway.

These forces all flow together. The genuine strains of inequality, whipped up in the media tornado, propel a sense of competition between people and societies—whether or not those differences are the actual cause. Here hybrid warfare enters again. The more effectively the aggressor can deepen those divides, the stronger the attack. If you impose sanctions, you want them to affect one part of your target society more than others. If you attack a power grid, you want to leave open questions about who ordered the attack to sow instability. Uncertainty creates domestic ambiguity about who the enemy is.

The resulting divides run along different identities in different societies. What we in the West see as the liberal-conservative split shows up in other societies as secular vs. religious, urban vs. rural, or ethnic divisions, to mention just a few. All can drive public opinion and shape how a state treats its allies, enemies, and neighbors. Heightened competition, and perhaps ultimately conflict, ends up as the result.

The solution requires leadership. All states need responsible leaders who foster cooperation and refrain from exploiting foreign conflict for domestic political gain. The world also needs multilateral structures strong enough to moderate tensions between states and find common solutions—because what we miss amid the blame game is that we all face the same problems.

Conclusion

In 2024 I sat next to South African President Cyril Ramaphosa at an international luncheon focused on conflict prevention. Among the first three speakers, not one mentioned the conflict in Sudan. Astonished, I turned to President Ramaphosa and said, "How is it possible that we're just talking about Ukraine and Israel?" He shook his head to express that he was not surprised.

Conflict is a collective problem. Its roots lie in our shared global challenges, and its reach can easily grow from regional to global. Yet the current world disorder only addresses conflict piecemeal. When security—along with trade, climate, energy, and so many critical global matters—becomes bilateral and transactional, the solutions are only local and rarely lasting. We need new systemic measures to address conflict, and these measures must account equitably for the needs and narratives of the Global West, East, and South.

As if we needed more reason, the fracturing of UN authority carries another, potentially existential, danger: the proliferation of nuclear weapons. Nine states (India, Pakistan, North Korea, Israel, and the five permanent UN Security Council members) are assumed to have acquired a nuclear arsenal. So far, broad consensus between West and East that the number should not rise—and that nuclear conflict would deliver catastrophic destruction on all—has held the threat in check. Now, as Putin rattles his saber and more states approach readiness to build a bomb, the equilibrium is under strain.

Where do these trends lead? In simple terms, we can see our challenge through the prism of three present conflicts: Russia's war against Ukraine (where the West expects but has not received global support), the Middle East (where the West's words and actions prove inconsistent), and Sudan (which the West largely ignores).

In both Ukraine and Gaza, we see an old conflict playing out on new local, regional, and global scales. We see high-tech warfare accompanied by sabotage, sanctions, and subversive social media campaigns. We see domestic pressures driving foreign policy choices. All these dynamics underscore the need for systemic measures to achieve and sustain peace.

The war in Ukraine has already sparked systemic shifts, inspiring new countries to join NATO and NATO to return to its roots as protector of European peace. As the war inches toward a conclusion, watch closely to answer essential questions: Who will broker an end? Which players will observe a ceasefire? Which issues remain unresolved? What structures will emerge to prevent a return to war? The answers for Ukraine ultimately will form the basis of a new European security order.

Both Ukraine and Gaza also underscore that the dividing lines between the Global West, East, and South are not clear—and that the West has work to do to regain the South's trust. Beyond the battlefields, both are wars of narratives and the proliferation of alternative concepts for defining and addressing the fight. For example, is the Gaza conflict a war on terrorism? A war between Israel and Hamas? Or Israel and Palestine? Or Arabs and Israelis? Or Israel and Iran? The answer depends on the frame.

In Sudan, a war between rival armed factions erupted in April 2023 and had killed tens of thousands of people and displaced more than 8 million by early 2025. The ongoing violence has driven the world's worst displacement crisis and largest hunger crisis. Yet in many countries of the Global West, it barely makes news. Until now, the Global West has wanted our wars to be the world's concern, but we haven't shown consummate concern with wars elsewhere. Therein lies a challenge to overcome.

Just as the global challenges of climate change, migration, and pandemics can only be met through collaboration, the same is true of modern conflicts. The foundations of the new world order are already under construction. In fact, the wars in Ukraine, Gaza, and Sudan may offer indications of its emerging form. The solutions we forge there will, in turn, set new standards for the international system. Let us make sure that those solutions engage other states as true partners, build institutions to last beyond this moment, and lead us toward the antidote to fragmentation: cooperation.

Cooperation

October 2024. I land in Beijing for my first state visit to China as president. A red carpet, schoolchildren with flags and flowers, and rows of uniformed soldiers greet me as I walk alongside President Xi Jinping.

It's a moment for classical diplomacy—made more urgent by global upheaval. I believe that diplomacy is human before strategic. The world works better through cooperation than conflict. And there are mutual benefits for those with the courage to engage.

Personality matters. I've always found President Xi easy to engage: serious but open, willing to listen. I tell him it feels good to stand here together representing almost 1.4 billion people. He laughs.

After the ceremony we talk for three and a half hours. My team has prepared thoroughly—with allies, clear goals, and hard questions. Ukraine is top of mind. I raise my concerns. Xi responds that his main concern is to prevent escalation, provocation, and expansion. "Isn't that," I ask, "exactly what North Korea is doing by sending ammunition and troops to Russia?" Xi quietly smiles.

These are the kinds of things you can say if you have a relationship of mutual respect.

Diplomacy is not binary. It is a tool to bridge differences. It requires compromise, patience, and humility. If I had entered with moral grandstanding, the meeting would have been brief—and final. Instead, we opened space for honesty and incremental progress. This was values-based realism and dignified foreign policy in action. And this, for the sake of the future world order, is what the West must do.

Let's talk about the weather. The year 2024 was crazy. Consider September alone. That month, Vietnam's strongest storm in seventy years buried towns and people under mud and damaged or destroyed more than 200,000 homes. Flash floods across central and southern Europe washed away buildings and sent tens of thousands of people fleeing their homes. And Hurricane Helene poured twenty-nine inches of rain on the US state of North Carolina, sweeping away small towns in areas not previously considered flood zones and causing more than $200 billion in damage. By the end of 2024, wildfires had consumed more than 7,000 square miles of Brazil, where severe drought seared tropical forest into a tinderbox. And as 2025 began, a wind-driven wildfire in Los Angeles not only threatened the edges of a major American city but consumed large swaths of the city itself.

Sadly, we have become used to such news. Climatic extremes routinely produce deadly and mind-boggling weather contrasts across the globe. These events also affect neighboring regions through impacts on ecosystems, agriculture, population flows, and supply chains.

The World Meteorological Organization (WMO) calculated that the number of extreme weather events causing large-scale disasters has increased fivefold during the past fifty years. Whether or not you believe in human-made climate change—and I strongly do—we must acknowledge that humankind's relation with nature has changed. As populations grew, we colonized flood plains, drained swamps, cut forests, burned fuel, straightened rivers and streams. Now we recognize, belatedly, that these changes put humans directly in the path of increasingly frequent and devastating climate events.

Climate change and extreme weather have become iconic examples of problems that not even the most strong-willed or self-sufficient country can tackle on its own. Others include the impacts of accelerating technology and changing demography, pandemics, financial system stability, terrorism, hunger relief, access to water, and global waste management. We can only address these challenges together.

The good news is that, despite competition and conflict, our own interests will necessarily drive us toward cooperation. The challenge is to do it right.

We have made considerable strides, at least on extreme weather events. While the number of natural disasters has increased, the global death toll is in decline. Information sharing and international forecasting have increased global preparedness. After a catastrophe, the international community races to provide technical support and humanitarian relief. Politically, the Paris Climate Accords of 2015 represented a significant success, as 195 states recognized that climate change requires a global effort. The US withdrawal puts a dent in this solidarity, but the direction has been set.

Global challenges are not only about crisis management but also better living conditions: access to communication, safe international travel, basic education, and more. Political scientists call these "global public goods" whose benefits or costs affect everyone, across borders.

Most countries recognize the imperative for cooperation and want to participate—and to wield influence. Watching the news it's easy to think international relations are anarchy. Yet in reality, countries are voting with their feet. Nine candidate states are queuing to join the EU, two for ASEAN, and many lobbying for a permanent UN Security Council seat. BRICS is adding members. In an age of assertive nationalism, countries nevertheless see value in cooperation.

Ultimately, the future global order will not be either-or. It will be characterized by competition and conflict as much as by cooperation. The need for global rules to manage the distribution and flow of global goods ensures that multilateralism will play an important role in restoring us to order. Yet its impact depends on how effectively we build it.

Liberal internationalists used to see international cooperation as a functional tool and a moral imperative. Today, the moral dimension seems an antiquated vestige. Democratization and human rights have become contested ideas between West, East, and South. When Western policymakers extol shared values they sound, to a global audience, somewhat off tune. Multilateralism for its own sake is doomed. Multilateralism must be shown to deliver.

The good news is there is plenty of opportunity for it to do so. Interests, not values, provide common ground. States across the spectrum from democracies to autocracies share goals like stability, prosperity, and economic growth. Global goods are indispensable assets to achieve these goals. And multilateral cooperation will be the indispensable tool to provide them. To illustrate what's at stake let's explore three examples: climate change, trade, and security.

Global Goods: Climate Change

Addressing climate change is a whole-society endeavor. The stakes include farmers' livelihoods, populations' food security, industries' energy supply, households' heating, mass mobility, and technological innovation. In our globalized world, environmental shocks in one country will likely have knock-on effects across the region.

Countries have different climate priorities depending on their own strengths and weaknesses, trade patterns, and political agendas. A small island nation may care most about sea-level mitigation, while mid-latitude countries seek to prevent wildfires and protect agriculture, and northern European states scramble to integrate climate-driven immigrants. This complexity makes multilateral climate negotiations difficult.

At the same time, they have proved fertile for innovating international cooperation and produced strategies that may be effective in realms beyond climate. The UN-sponsored Paris Climate Accords introduced voluntary commitments to reduce carbon emissions instead of the 1997 Kyoto Protocol's legally binding ones. This allowed more countries to join, including high emitters such as the US and China who rejected legal obligations. Voluntary commitments provide leeway to adjust to national needs. But the increased reporting duties, Nationally Determined Contributions (NDCs), and political capital invested create public pressure to follow through.

The Paris Accords also bolstered the principle of a "common but differentiated responsibility." Many developing countries argued that Western nations today enjoy the advantages of the industrialization that contributed most of the world's historic emissions. Therefore, they reasoned, industrialized nations should shoulder a greater share of the reduction. Without directly confirming such views, the EU and US reacted by putting large premiums on green technologies, seeking to make climate policies a driver of innovation and growth.

Climate-friendly development has also become a key element in global development efforts. The EU's Global Gateway infrastructure initiative makes environmental sustainability a central priority. China's Belt and Road Initiative now emphasizes ecosystem protection, a shift its promoters cheer as an unfolding "Green Silk Road." The results of such ambitions remain to be seen. But they clearly mark a field of growing cooperation.

Despite these positive steps, however, climate cooperation has far to go. The litmus test may lie in providing adequate finance for developing countries to reach their national climate action goals. In 2009, high-income countries collectively promised $100 billion per year from 2020 onward. They have not yet provided much of it. Plus, many of the funds that did arrive were structured as loans rather than grants, which further contributes to low-income countries' heavy debt burden.

What's at stake here is the credibility of high-income Western countries in the Global South. Many developing countries are disproportionately exposed to climate risks. They naturally perceive failures of support as hypocrisy against the background of continuous calls for a common global effort.

What is equally at stake, of course, is the success of global climate action itself. Decarbonizing Western economies will not make enough impact if developing economies build growth on dirty energy—and collaboration is critical to prevent the latter. Recurrent crises will also require emergency responses and will produce economic ripple effects and migration. If the Global South remains exposed to climate risks, the West will inevitably share in paying the price.

Global Goods: Trade
The size of the global economy has roughly tripled since the Cold War ended. Average per capita income has nearly doubled. Over a billion people were lifted from poverty. The volume of global trade in goods also expanded almost fivefold between 1995 and 2022—and this is no coincidence. Trade remains a key driver of global growth and as such is an essential global good.

A series of events, however, has limited trade expansion over the past decade or so. The global financial crisis and ensuing euro-crisis slowed general economic growth. The pandemic put imports out of fashion amid supply-chain interruptions and fears that import dependency could undermine economic resilience. Russia's invasion of Ukraine exposed Western Europe's overreliance on Russian energy and deepened the aversion to global trade. Friendshoring and a growing abandonment of the "just-in-time" economy (which relied on fast trading routes to deliver goods precisely when needed) rose in its wake.

Digital technology has simultaneously pushed trade in both positive and negative directions. Ecommerce and expanded digital networks make international division of labor easier and thus potentially fuel trade. Yet the digital transformation has also left workers in more traditional industries behind, creating resentment against globalization. From resentment grew populism, which often promotes economic protectionism—and thus ironically ends up hindering the domestic growth it champions.

These kinds of reactionary moves against trade present a threat that we must collaboratively address. Fragmentation, or even deglobalization, may result from accumulating risks and fears. For now, former WTO Director-General Pascal Lamy argues that global trade remains strong. At the same time, he warned in *Foreign Affairs* in 2022 that the sum of all fears could drive precautionary measures up to the degree that "deglobalization could become a self-fulfilling prophecy."

In trade, as in climate, nations can make limited progress alone, especially small and medium-sized countries. Multilateral cooperation is the only viable option. Yet the WTO, which has enabled global liberalization of trade since its creation in 1995, has recently appeared paralyzed. Negotiations to lower trade barriers and reform the international trading system have run aground. The so-called "Doha Development Agenda," meant to support developing economies, is not progressing. The WTO's dispute settlement mechanism is defunct. New rules on digital trade and intellectual property rights have not found consensus.

The WTO's stagnation is exacerbated by global competition. Since Western countries benefited from WTO-led globalization, developing countries today naturally demand differential support to level the playing field. The US and EU in turn sharply criticize that China—one of the biggest winners of globalization—still profits from its formal status as a "developing country" within the WTO. The WTO used to be able to forge trade cooperation despite its member states' differing geopolitical ambitions. Not anymore.

Global fragmentation here, as in so many realms, leads to regionalization. One example is the USMCA trade agreement, previously known as NAFTA, that covers North America from Mexico to Canada. The EU also has agreements linking the Common Market with third countries. Regional trade agreements exist on all continents. The downside is that they exclude others and undermine the WTO's requirement to treat all trading partners equally. Regional trade agreements are the economic equivalent of geopolitical bloc building. In the wrong circumstances they risk cementing cleavages rather than furthering cooperation.

The dangers of this situation are twofold. First, the WTO remains the single most important forum to address structural challenges and set rules for ecommerce, digital trade, and data governance. It remains indispensable to prevent protectionism and help developing countries update their economies. Making trade a pillar of a global economic recovery requires a functioning, active WTO—and trade is unlikely to thrive without one.

That scenario will, in turn, contribute to rising geopolitical tensions between West, East, and South. And if more antitrade policies result, they will only push geopolitical conflicts deeper into the economic realm until geopolitical and economic tensions become mutually reinforcing.

Maybe even more than with climate, a rules-based international order may rise or fall with the health of a rules-based trading order. We already see signs of weakness. The weaponization of economic tools against adversaries like Russia or Iran causes doubts within the Global South about the West's reliability in keeping faith with such an order. The US refusal to cooperate on reforming the WTO's conflict resolution mechanism allows critics once more to accuse the West of hypocrisy—upholding an international system only as long as it serves its interests. WTO reform may serve as the Global South's bellwether on whether the West will fixate only on besting China or rebuild an international system more responsive to the needs of all.

Global Goods: Security
Security seems to be the least likely field of international cooperation—as a land war rages in Ukraine, the war in Gaza continues to take a devastating toll, the consequences of the Israel-Iran escalation remain uncertain, and conflicts elsewhere seem intractable. Yet peace is the ultimate global public good. And it has a track record of giving birth to unexpected breakthroughs.

One of them is non-proliferation. During the Cold War, the 1968 Treaty on the Non-Proliferation of Nuclear Weapons and the 1972 Anti-Ballistic Missile Treaty were milestones that provided stability between the two superpowers. The Chemical Weapons Convention and the Strategic Arms Reductions Treaty (START) in the 1990s were part of the peace dividend after the Cold War.

But as if to mark the new epoch, recent years have produced no good news on non-proliferation. In 2019, the US withdrew from the Intermediate-Range Nuclear Forces Treaty, signed in 1987, citing a Russian lack of compliance. Russia left the Comprehensive Nuclear-Test Ban Treaty and the Treaty on Conventional Armed Forces in Europe in 2023. Now New START, one of the last major non-proliferation treaties, is due to expire in 2026.

All these treaties involved parties suspicious of each other and antagonistic in their interests. Only patient diplomacy behind the scenes allowed them to find compromises that made them—and the world—safer. Today would be a good moment for another major diplomatic breakthrough—and the leadership to sustain it.

Multilateral institutions also continue to play a vital role for global security. The International Atomic Energy Agency was indispensable in monitoring Iran's compliance with the nuclear deal. In Ukraine, it gained access to the Zaporizhzhia power plant seized by Russian forces, which was in acute danger amid the fighting. The UN proper remains pivotal in promoting a peaceful use of outer space and preventing the stationing of weapons of mass destruction in earth's orbit.

Regional organizations are important security providers, too. The EU, for example, deploys around 3,500 military and 1,300 civilians on three continents to support peacekeeping, capacity building, and regional stability. Western Africa's ECOWAS has executed robust military missions in several crises. Even if conflict persists, ECOWAS's credibility as a regional player is a key asset in promoting stability.

Amid global disorder we also take for granted the many unglamorous successes in international police cooperation, anti-trafficking, and intelligence sharing. We would be in a worse place without such quiet efforts. On the other hand, security is an indivisible good; if one region lacks security, the neighbors and the neighbors' neighbors cannot live in peace.

Global Rules

Countless countries have called to reform the multilateral system since the UN's founding in 1945. It is time to realize that such reform is not a political project but an ongoing process.

Over eight decades, the international system has changed in too many ways to count. International organizations proliferated and participating countries multiplied. Scores of NGOs created a parallel network of international cooperation, often closely linked with states. The UN itself, though not conceived for this purpose by its founders, proved instrumental in consolidating the statehood of decolonized countries in the 1960s and 1970s. Then a new majority of developing countries helped shift the UN's focus from political and civil rights to social and economic ones. Financial institutions moved from postwar reconstruction to development.

The lesson is that time and again, institutions of international cooperation have changed in response to the challenges of the time. It is time for another update, and a meaningful one. Successful cooperation rests on establishing and staying faithful to a fresh set of global agreements, forged by a more equal voice among countries.

How to craft those rules is another question. Eight decades of evolution have produced so thick a layer of multilateralism that a complete overhaul is but a theoretical idea. I would even argue that a tabula rasa is undesirable, as it would hurl us quickly into chaos and abandon many multilateral tools worth keeping. We should aim instead for incremental change while maintaining the flexibility to use more fluid, spontaneous forms of multilateral cooperation to respond to specific challenges. A "less is more" motto would enable us to keep using those parts of the system that function and facilitate dialogue even while pursuing reform.

This incremental change should be built on a minimum of rules and one overarching goal. The rules relate to the rule of law and respect for human rights. The goal relates to representation.

Let's start with the rules. In an age of division and mistrust, a values-based foreign policy has become difficult to sustain. To resolve conflict, we need to engage players with whom we—speaking from the perspective of Western democracy—have little worldview in common. We won't get far by projecting liberal democratic ideals onto them. Instead, the first rule to promote should be respect for and protection of international law and treaties. The rule of law on the international plane means staying true to the principle expressed in Latin as *pacta sunt servanda*, or "agreements must be kept." There is no point in dialogue and compromise if there is no assurance that parties will keep their agreements. Abandonment of this rule means a step further toward anarchy. On the other hand, any notion of international order will find solid footing in this principle.

This is why the retreat of the United States from agreements like the Paris Climate Accords poses a dilemma. It allows the opponents of a rules-based order to argue that the West's foremost country betrayed the very order the West tries to protect.

This is also why the weaponization of trade, finance, travel, and other elements of global interdependence is a double-edged sword. We are quick to call for sanctions against certain international actors. But the EU acts prudently when it scrupulously examines whether its sanctions are in accord with international law. Punishing rogue states may be our heartfelt desire. But imposing sanctions without grounding in international law means enshrining the principle that might makes right. It kills the incentive for anybody else to make shared rules, if rules do not promise to restrain the power of the powerful.

Pushing human rights as a global value will prove as fraught as promoting democratization. The core body of human rights laws is enshrined in the UN Charter of 1945 and the Universal Declaration of Human Rights in 1948. But despite broad global recognition, its interpretation and enforcement remains controversial. And amid criticisms of double standards and selective application, the West would be doomed to failure if it wanted to police respect for human rights around the world.

The conclusion need not be to abandon the human rights agenda. The rights outlined in the UN Charter and the UDHR still provide an indispensable compass for international relations. However, it might be wiser and more credible if Western commentators employ less of a professorial attitude when judging human rights situations elsewhere. Western governments cannot stop talking to governments with poor human rights records. Instead, an incentive-driven approach might improve rights more effectively than applying conditionality to Western cooperation.

If respect for international law and human rights should be the minimum consensus for global reform, a fairer distribution of voice and representation should be the outcome. Shared values should remain a goal but not a condition of collaboration. The legitimacy, and thereby durability, of any order hinges on the perception of most actors that they stand on equal footing. States will only believe in institutions if they have agency in them.

In September 2024, I made my own proposal for UN Security Council reform in a speech at the UN General Assembly. My proposal contains three critical elements. One, that all major continents should always be represented. I find it unacceptable that there is no representation from Latin America or Africa, and that China alone represents Asia. I also question the fact that Europe is represented by three states, one of which, Russia, is blatantly violating everything the UN stands for.

My proposed remedy is to double the permanent members to ten, adding one from Latin America, two from Africa and two from Asia, plus ten seats for rotating members. Second, I propose that no single state should have a Security Council veto. I understand why this rule was established after World War II, but in today's world it simply obstructs decision-making. Third, I contend that any Security Council member that violates the UN Charter should have its voting rights suspended.

It is telling that in a room of UN ambassadors from around the world, my proposals received a hearty applause. Well, at least from 188 members out of 193.

Beyond the UN system we might need a more flexible, demand-driven, and sometimes regional approach to navigate today's disorder. Efforts by the EU, African Union, Mercosur, ASEAN, and others to pool sovereignty on trade and security are prime examples. What may look like fragmentation could turn out to be a pragmatic way to put the global community back on a path toward order.

Successful reform also requires a turn toward a *dignified foreign policy*, which I describe as the willingness to listen to each other with an open mind and greater appreciation of differences between societies, cultures, regions, and states. This is a task for East, West, and South alike. But if the US, EU, and their partners in the Global West seek international leadership, they need to lead by example.

Triangle of Power
Beyond the playing fields of economics and politics, the global contest also extends into the judges' box and league headquarters. With the international order in flux, East, South, and West are carrying competition into the realm of international cooperation itself. The new world order is the winner's prize.

The existing international system provides the venue for this contest. But only in part, as new forms and places of cooperation emerge and grow.

For the foreseeable future, Russia and China will continue their twin offensive to change the international landscape. They have shared the goal of a multipolar world order (and tacitly, deposing the US) since they proclaimed it in the Sino-Russian declaration of 1997. Yet they differ in their strategies. Russia, through its exports of energy, weaponry, and nuclear technology, remains an indispensable partner for many, often poor and autocratic, countries. China plays the economic card. Tactically, Russia is more disruptive, exploiting crisis and conflict to drain Western resources. China is more constructive. It promotes its own visions of global order and creates new venues, while also pushing reform from within the existing system.

The Global South is somewhat agnostic about the future order—provided it is a clear improvement from the current one. It shares the East's aim to make the system less dependent on the West. But it does not want to replace dependency on one power center with dependency on another. For the time being, the South is likely to continue to hedge its bets, exploiting its ability to court both East and West and extract benefits from both. It will accept and draw on regionalization without letting up the pressure on global institutions.

The Global West finds itself in a complex situation. To preserve the international order, it must change. And while it may be the camp with the greatest convergence of interests, values, and goals, Europe and the US differ fundamentally on one issue. For Europe, multipolarity is inscribed in its history. Europe is used to internal differences, multiple power centers, changing patterns of dominance, and the hard labor of compromise. The US prefers a world of clear contrasts; bipolarity is its natural framework for strategic thinking. Its National Security Strategy clearly defines one main competitor, China, and ranks every other second or third.

The advantage of the US approach is that it calls out the Chinese power grab as China continues its stealthy ascent to global leadership. The downside is that both the US and China deliberately choose confrontation with each other over cooperation on an increasing number of issues. This bipolar stance, in turn, freezes relations with the Global South in their historic state, as a derivative of great power competition.

Europe and the EU take a more moderate position. To protect its trade interests, the EU recognizes China as a systemic rival and economic competitor but also as a potential partner. And the EU realizes that it cannot sufficiently protect its security, not even in its immediate neighborhood, without strong support from the US. Together, the EU and its member states have the widest reaching and most densely knit diplomatic network around the globe, making Europe uniquely placed to help find compromise on any topic in any region in the world.

The big plot twist for the Global West is the second Trump administration. Through tariffs, treaty cancellations, and claims on other countries' territory, the US has moved dramatically toward transactionalism. The ultimate duration and impact of this trend remains to be seen. If it continues, however, it could make global cooperation more patchwork, interest-based, and á la carte. With the US out of the game, the EU would have to seek more bilateral deals with the rest of the world. As it now holds more than forty trade agreements with more than seventy countries, it already has a head start. We also can't exclude the possibility that the Trump administration's startup-like "move fast and break things" approach will eventually lead to new agreements and better practices, such as more even burden sharing on security.

In the big picture, the way to win the world-order contest is for the Global West first to be proactive in reforming existing institutions, with an eye on the Global South's demands. Second, it needs flexibility to engage partners, competitors, and adversaries in the forum best suited for the issue at hand. Some actors will be partners on one issue and competitors or even adversaries on others. This combination of reliability and flexibility will open a path to preserve elements of the current world order while growing new parts to accommodate the demands and ambitions of a changing world.

Conclusion
It is easy to point to all the disappointments of our international institutions today. The WHO failed on vaccine provision, the WTO is paralyzed on trade negotiations, the IMF and World Bank cannot mitigate the debt distress of the least-developed countries, and most of all, the UN Security Council is unable to preserve peace. Amid this disarray, European Council on Foreign Relations Senior Policy Fellow Jana Puglierin recently described multilateral institutions as the "Potemkin villages of today."

I disagree. We must not throw the baby out with the bathwater. The UN, for example, plays a vital role in development, climate policies, the limiting of biological and chemical weapons, non-proliferation, and many more fields. It continues to serve as a valuable crisis manager. It helped negotiate the Black Sea Grain Initiative, permitting critical food and fertilizer exports via Ukraine even amid war, and its relief organizations provide aid around the globe. The UN remains a forum to initiate discussions on new themes like artificial intelligence and cybersecurity. And it has an important task in protecting sovereignty and statehood. It may not always be as effective as we want it to be, but we would be much worse off without it.

We need to manage our expectations. The UN won't resolve the war in Ukraine or the Middle East, the World Bank won't cover for all the costly climate policies. And no institution, agreement, or single great power will be able to control all conflict and competition. International cooperation can, however, *influence* competition and conflict. It can help us manage them—provided we approach it with the humility to listen and the flexibility to adapt.

We are at a tipping point. Action to update the international system is urgent. The longer the West ignores this reality, the more cooperation becomes local and regional and thus prone to fragmentation and conflict. The sooner we reform the system, the greater our chances of preserving an ordered, cooperative world.

Conclusions

March 2025. Three years and three weeks since Russia started its full-scale war of aggression against Ukraine. Many expected the war to be over in three days. But Putin made a colossal tactical and strategic mistake. And Ukraine has put up a heroic fight.

My wife Suzanne and I are hosting a private dinner at our home in Helsinki. We have two very special guests: Volodymyr Zelenskyy and Olena Zelenska. It is a rare moment for them to take a breath amid their fight for survival.

The war is at a stalemate; we call it a war of attrition. Russia's territorial advances in the first half of 2025 are as abysmal as the human casualties are colossal. It has gained only 0.25 percent of Ukrainian territory so far this year. Meanwhile, casualties are up to the thousands each day.

Earlier this afternoon, Finns thronged the streets to show support for Ukraine. Zelenskyy took a phone call with President Trump. We were, we hoped, working toward peace.

It's just the four of us now. Jazz in the background. Candles on the table. We talk about our children and how their family has coped with the stress of war. Suzanne and I are full of admiration for their tenacity and courage. We Finns understand what Ukraine is going through.

I remember my text message exchange with Lavrov. Russia has again shown its colors: imperialist ambitions and disdain for human life and international law. It is a former great power in decline, gasping for the remnants of what used to be. But as a Finn I never underestimate Russia.

The easy solution for the rest of us would be to cave in, but we simply can't. Ukraine has not, and it won't. When one nation tries to change the world order by force, it has consequences for every nation on earth.

All of us have a choice. We can engage or disengage.

I began writing this book when Donald Trump was ending his first term as US president. I finished writing it when Trump was beginning his second term. That leap alone, over just four years, illustrates how much the world has changed.

In fact, the world has changed more in the past three years than in the previous thirty years combined. Making sense of it has been like trying to hit a moving target. Yet writing has helped clarify my view of the big picture. Returning to political office has done the same. My experience as president has strengthened my belief that values-based realism, combined with dignified foreign policy, should be the Global West's response. It has also affirmed for me that regional integration, paired with the rejuvenation of international institutions, is the best path toward global peace, stability, and security.

The more world leaders I meet, and the more classified and unclassified analyses I read, the more convinced I am that the Global South will decide the new balance of power. History, geography, and demographics are on the side of these rising states. I am also convinced that after a period of disorder, some kind of new order *will* emerge. As we take up our roles in shaping it, the following is what we must all understand.

A Glimpse of the Future

The postwar institutions that have helped steer the world through its most rapid development and have sustained a period of relative peace still stand the test of time. But to survive, they must change. First, because a world based on competition without cooperation will lead to conflict. It will also lead us away from the solutions we all need. Second, because states that lack agency in the existing system will disinvest in it. And who can blame them? Third, because the new world order will not wait. It is already clear that transactional and multipolar disorder feeds conflict and chaos. The chips are falling. Timing, as well as strategy, makes a difference in the direction the world goes.

I foresee at least *three* scenarios that could emerge in the decade ahead.

The first, disorder, would resemble what we have today. There would still be elements of the old order left, but respect for international rules and institutions would be à la carte and mostly based on interests—not innate values. The capacity to solve major challenges would remain limited, but the world at least would not devolve into greater chaos.

The second scenario is collapse. Here, the foundations of the liberal international order—rules and institutions—would continue to erode. The world would move closer to chaos without a clear nexus of power or the capacity to solve acute crises such as famines, pandemics, or conflicts. In this scenario, strongmen, warlords, or non-state actors would fill power vacuums. Stability and predictability would be the exception, not the norm. The danger is that local conflicts could spill into widespread war.

The third scenario is a rebalanced world order based on a new symmetry of power among the Global West, East, and South. This scenario has the potential to contain competition and nudge the world toward cooperation on climate, security, and technology—critical challenges that none of us can solve alone. This outcome is what this book is about.

The wild card for the Global West in any of these scenarios will be whether the United States actually wants to preserve a multilateral world order. The wild card for the Global East will be how China plays its hand on the world stage. The black swan for everyone would be the unlikeliest of alliances, a pact between the US, China, and Russia—between three strongmen—leaving the rest of us behind. In this world, power would rest at three poles: Trump, Xi, and Putin.

Trump's reelection undoubtedly affects the West's potential to influence a new world order. Yet no matter how inflamed the transatlantic relationship becomes, I do not believe that the core of it, NATO, will be weakened. On the contrary, it might be strengthened, not least because President Trump has pressured European members to increase their defense spending—which I consider healthy, at least under present circumstances. The challenge for a new world order will be Trump's reservations about international institutions and his affinity for tariffs, which ultimately harm not only their target countries but the US and everyone else. His early language on territorial acquisition also throws the reliability of sovereignty into question. World leaders should not necessarily take him literally on this, but we should take him seriously.

The most important lesson to draw is that states—including small states like mine—are not bystanders in the story. The new order will be determined by decisions taken by political leaders, whether democrats, autocrats, or something in between. And here a particular responsibility falls on the Global West as the architect of the passing order and still, economically and militarily, the most powerful global group. The way we carry that mantle matters.

The Road to Helsinki
It is clarifying to view the global shakeup through three lenses: values, interests, and power. Foreign policy is usually a mix of all three. Right now, all are changing. Values are less universal than we expected. Interests shift in real time. Power is changing hands—between the US and China, and into the hands of midsize nations. You could say that the US emphasis is shifting from values to interests, China from interests to power, and Russia from power to interests. The evolving order forces even the biggest players to change.

Coming from a small state, I understand that I can play on the field of values *and* interests. The power I have is limited. But even small states that play their cards right can be power brokers. They might not have the power, but they have the power to influence.

My foreign policy approach is values-based realism, which gives space to all to navigate a world of difficult trade-offs. Are you willing to compromise your values if it is in your interests? Or will you stay true to your values even if doing so defies your interests? Are you willing to compromise your individual interests for the good of the whole? War emerges often from an innate and stubborn belief that you are right. Preserving peace requires compromise.

I do not suggest that liberal democracies should sacrifice core democratic values and beliefs on the altar of power, influence, and realpolitik. These values will always serve as a stronger basis for success than pure interests. Would I like to persuade the rest of the world to be more Finnish or perhaps Nordic? Yes! Because I believe the system of governance we have up North has proven itself. Open, free, just, and equal societies work. Values should be part of the conversation. But we cannot, and should not, seek to impose ours on others.

In fact, if a choice between values and realism must be made, the Global South will have the tiebreaking vote. Yet the South does not want to make a binary choice between a democratic West and an authoritarian East. Were the South obliged to choose, it would probably gravitate toward Europe and North America. There are not long queues of migrants waiting to cross borders into Russia, China, or North Korea. The South wants, however, to make that choice on its own terms. And it is in the global interest to let them.

Realistic Reasons to Be Optimistic

Like many heads of state, the president of Finland delivers a New Year's speech. In 2025, I shared this observation: "It is easy to list what is wrong and to concentrate on threats. It is much harder to find solutions. Pessimism leads to inaction, optimism to action, realism to solutions." This is true across borders.

As president I will continue to work for a world that I perceive to be just, fair, and functional. I will do so based on my inherently Western values while recognizing that not everyone shares them. Be that as it may, I make here three concrete proposals that I believe will be useful to all in rebalancing a new world order—and convincing leaders across the globe that it is necessary and urgent to do so.

First, there is no such thing as a perfect system of governance, but I firmly believe that open, free, and democratic societies are the basis for national success. There is a reason why liberal democracies top almost all global rankings, from quality of life to GDP per capita to life expectancy. The decentralization of power allows corrective measures to renew progress and development. Authoritarian regimes simply do not have the capacity to react to change in the long run. Freedom always trumps control.

I do not claim that authoritarian states are incapable of creating welfare and prosperity, but that all models of governance that limit freedom will only survive in the short to medium term. Natural resources, demography, and size can only take you so far; authoritarian regimes ultimately hit a wall and are forced into more radical change. Autocrats, likewise, tend to leave office in one of three ways: in jail, in exile, or in a coffin. At the same time, democracies must understand that their model of society is not an end state. It is a process that must be constantly protected and developed.

My second proposal is that states should strengthen regional cooperation. I am fully aware that geography, history, and culture differ everywhere, but regional integration is both in states' national interest and a useful segue to global cooperation. There is a direct correlation between prosperity and regional cooperation. My personal experience stems from the Nordics, OSCE, the

European Union, and NATO—which, despite their complexities, have generally delivered peace, stability, and prosperity.

My third and final proposal is about the most important international organization in the world, the United Nations. There are others, such as the World Bank, IMF, and WTO, that need rebalancing, but the most important reform linked to peace and stability is at the UN. The specific changes I endorse are those I outlined in my UN General Assembly speech in 2024:

1. Expand the Security Council to include five additional permanent members (one from Latin America, two from Africa, and two from Asia), plus ten rotating members.

2. Eliminate single-state veto power.

3. Suspend the voting rights of any Security Council member that violates the UN Charter.

When I made this proposal, I could hear the applause of 188 out of 193 members. But I did not see current Security Council members clapping. Unsurprisingly, they did not want to dilute their dominant position. Yet unless they accept the need to rebalance power, they will forfeit the chance to choose.

Long Live the Triangle of Power

I began the book by noting that this is the 1918, 1945, and 1989 moment of our generation. Or perhaps it is all of them put into one? But there is no such thing as deterministic foreign policy. Humans make foreign policy. Every day. It is a choice.

The future order presents a critical role for each part of the world to play. In the competition for the Global South's support it would be a mistake for the West to rely only on the appeal of freedom and democracy. The East would be equally mistaken to think that big infrastructure projects and generous credit buy it unchecked influence. The South has plenty of options.

For the Global West, values-based realism and dignified foreign policy should mean adopting a new, more cooperative framework with the South. Rather than coercion we should deploy persuasion: setting an example that others may adopt. This entails collaborative partnerships as well as changed behavior. The charge from the Global South of Western double standards is sometimes deafening. The way to persuade is to live up to our principles. This also means recrafting a global system where the rules and norms are not just adopted but also created by the South, forging trade agreements on equal footing, sharing technological data and knowledge, and cooperating on defense and infrastructure. The cooperation need not be transactional, but many Global South countries can provide clear benefits in raw materials or security.

In its relationship with the Global East, the West must acknowledge the difference in values and interests but also understand that decoupling permanently is not sustainable. Economic interdependence is too deeply rooted. So too is the need to act collaboratively to confront climate change and other shared challenges. The West can stay true to its values but cooperate where its interests apply. There is nothing to be gained from lecturing the Global East, but the West can point to real-world evidence. China's economic ascent has been based on liberal markets, capitalism, and free trade, along with an ample workforce.

Russia has failed to match that pace because it has not used market mechanisms to modernize its economy.

At some point the West may start to rebuild a relationship with Russia—but in my mind only when it ends its brutal war in Ukraine, takes responsibility for the war, and credibly commits to international rules and order.

The opportunity for the Global South lies in leveling the economic playing field. Stark inequality remains across the South, but technology, properly managed and used, provides competitive opportunities for all. There is no need for nations in this group to choose between West and East. They might note, however, that open, free, and democratic societies work better than closed, controlled, and authoritarian states. Freedom is an engine of prosperity. States where leaders cling to power are usually on a road to stagnation.

Not only diplomats but also everyday civilians have a role to play. Global cooperation is not a spectator sport. Neither is democracy. It requires participation: voting, standing for election, participating in local boards and decision-making bodies, demanding the best from our representatives. Our democratic systems will not last forever if we do not cherish and develop them.

The world above all needs the capacity to look forward in a spirit of mutual respect and cooperation. No one should doubt our ability to meet the obstacles ahead if the world's three spheres—West, East, and South—build a global order that respects difference and allows states to set their national interests in a broader framework of international cooperation. We should have no illusions, though, about the costs of failure. The first half of the twentieth century was warning enough.

"What humans begin, humans can also end."

So said my mentor, Finnish President and Nobel Peace Prize laureate Martti Ahtisaari. And so it is true of our intentional, essential world order. Humans created it in a time of critical need. Humans can allow it to erode into obsolescence. Or we can remodel it to begin anew.

FURTHER READING

Applebaum, Anne. *Twilight of Democracy: The Seductive Lure of Authoritarianism*. New York: Doubleday, 2020.

Bradford, Anu. *Digital Empires: The Global Battle to Regulate Technology*. New York: Oxford University Press, 2023.

Bremmer, Ian. *The Power of Crisis: How Three Threats—and Our Response—Will Change the World*. New York: Simon & Schuster, 2022.

Friedman, Thomas L. *The World Is Flat: A Brief History of the Twenty-First Century*. New York: Farrar, Straus and Giroux, 2005.

Fukuyama, Francis. *The End of History and the Last Man*. New York: Free Press, 1992. Reprint, London: Penguin Books, 2012.

Gessen, Masha. *The Man Without a Face: The Unlikely Rise of Vladimir Putin*. New York: Riverhead Books, 2012.

Grant, Adam. *Think Again: The Power of Knowing What You Don't Know*. London: WH Allen, 2021.

Harari, Yuval Noah. *Sapiens: A Brief History of Humankind*. New York: Harper, 2015.

Kahneman, Daniel. *Thinking, Fast and Slow*. New York: Farrar, Straus and Giroux, 2011.

Kennedy, Paul. *The Rise and Fall of the Great Powers: Economic Change and Military Conflict from 1500 to 2000*. New York: Random House, 1987.

Kissinger, Henry. *World Order*. New York: Penguin Press, 2014.

Leonard, Mark. *The Age of Unpeace: How Connectivity Causes Conflict*. London: Penguin Books, 2021.

Levitsky, Steven, and Daniel Ziblatt. *How Democracies Die*. New York: Crown, 2018.

Marshall, Tim. *Prisoners of Geography: Ten Maps That Tell You Everything You Need to Know About Global Politics*. London: Elliott and Thompson, 2015.

Moyo, Dambisa. *Dead Aid: Why Aid Is Not Working and How There Is a Better Way for Africa*. New York: Farrar, Straus and Giroux, 2009.

Papaconstantinou, George. *Whatever It Takes: The Battle for Post-Crisis Europe*. Athens: Papadopoulos Publishing, 2016.

Rosling, Hans, Ola Rosling, and Anna Rosling Rönnlund. *Factfulness: Ten Reasons We're Wrong About the World—and Why Things Are Better Than You Think.* New York: Flatiron Books, 2018.

Rudd, Kevin. *The Avoidable War: The Dangers of a Catastrophic Conflict Between the U.S. and Xi Jinping's China.* New York: PublicAffairs, 2022.

Thaler, Richard H., and Cass R. Sunstein. *Nudge: The Final Edition.* London: Penguin Books, 2021.

Zakaria, Fareed. *The Post-American World: Release 2.0.* New York: W.W. Norton, 2011.

ACKNOWLEDGMENTS

Writing a book is always a long process. It feels especially long when you are writing about international relations in the middle of a shift in the global power balance. Just when you think it is a wrap, things change again.

I started writing this book exactly five years ago, as a professor at the European University Institute in Florence. I finished writing it in summer 2025, in my second year as the thirteenth president of the Republic of Finland. When I began, I did not realize how much the world would change, let alone that I would reenter the stage of world politics, which I had left—permanently, I thought—in 2016.

I know it is rather unusual for a head of state to publish an analysis of international relations at the beginning of his or her term of office, but I felt that I had a story to tell. A story of academic analysis and practical experience—a look from the outside in and inside out. This book is not Finland's foreign policy doctrine; it is my personal take on how international relations have evolved since the Cold War and where we might be heading in the decades to come. World events will continue to roll on. This book should be read not only as an analysis of the past and present but a call for action into the future—a defense of democracy, multilateralism, and the liberal world order.

The book does not contain a bibliography or footnotes. I wanted it to be a journey of how my thinking has evolved from my days as a student of international relations in the immediate aftermath of the Cold War to my time as president amid a changing world order. I did not want the book to become a mammoth tome full of references, but I hope it shows my appreciation for all the people, books, and articles that have taught me so much over the years.

Writing a book is always a lonely job, but you can never do it alone. The biggest thanks for finalizing the manuscript go to my editor, Grace Rubenstein. For over a year, we worked together to get the book over the goal line. To put it simply: "No Grace = No Book." The biggest thanks for getting me started go to Jonas Brendebach, who was my research assistant in Florence (and is now a diplomat in the Auswärtiges Amt). He did a lot of the research and heavy lifting, especially on chapters 3, 6, and 9. Many thanks also to legendary *Financial Times* columnist Philip Stephens for substantive edits and challenging my arguments.

The book will come out in many different languages—thank you, Kirsi Koskinen, for keeping it all together. My book agent, Jim Levine, showed me how books get published around the world. The book has gone through many rounds of comments—thank you, Mark Leonard, Fabrizio Tassinari, George Papaconstantinou, Simon Hix, Erik Jones, Adam Grant, Brent Nelsen, Samir Saran, Kristiina Mäkelä, Timo Miettinen, Tuomas Forsberg, Risto E. J. Penttilä, Antti Helanterä, Aliisa Tornberg, and all of my friends and colleagues who did not want to be named publicly. A final word of thanks goes to my family, who have had to listen to me go on about the book for five years. Kiitos, tack for your patience. And as always, responsibility for the content of the book lies solely with the author.

I dedicate this book to the memory of President Martti Ahtisaari, to peace.

Alexander Stubb
Helsinki, June 2025

Columbia Global Reports is a nonprofit publishing imprint from Columbia University that commissions authors to produce works of original thinking and on-site reporting from all over the world, on a wide range of topics. Our books are short—novella-length, and readable in a few hours—but ambitious. They offer new ways of looking at and understanding the major issues of our time. Most readers are curious and busy. Our books are for them.

If this book changed the way you look at the world, and if you would like to support our mission, consider making a gift to Columbia Global Reports to help us share new ideas and stories.

Visit globalreports.columbia.edu to support our upcoming books, subscribe to our newsletter, and learn more about Columbia Global Reports. Thank you for being part of our community of readers and supporters.

Losing Big: America's Reckless Bet on Sports Gambling
Jonathan D. Cohen

Why Live: How Suicide Becomes an Epidemic
Helen C. Epstein

The Milk Tea Alliance: Inside Asia's Struggle Against Autocracy and Beijing
Jeffrey Wasserstrom

The Web Beneath the Waves: The Fragile Cables That Connect Our World
Samanth Subramanian

The Fall of Affirmative Action: Race, the Supreme Court, and the Future of Diversity in America
Justin Driver

The Robe and the Sword: How Buddhist Extremism Is Shaping Modern Asia
Sonia Faleiro